Whispers of Hope

BETH MOORE

With photographs by
Nicholas Pavloff & J.D. Marston

LifeWay Press
Nashville, Tennessee

Unless otherwise noted, Scripture quotations are from the Holy Bible,
New International Version, copyright © 1973, 1978, 1984
by International Bible Society.

Scripture quotations marked KJV are from the *King James Version.*

Printed in the United States of America

LifeWay Press
127 Ninth Avenue, North
Nashville, Tennessee 37234-0151

Nicolas Pavloff has photographed Asia, Europe,
the Pacific Rim, and North America. His work has appeared
in national and international publications. His work blends
the western U.S. landscape with ageless Oriental insight.
For further information, call 510-452-2468.

J.D. Marston, a former monk, is a recipient of the Ansel
Adams Award. The desire to demonstrate the presence of
God in nature is the primary motivation for his art.
For further information, call 719-256-4162.

Art Direction & Design: Edward A. Crawford

Bright Morning Star
God's diamond brooch
Upon the blackest night

Whispering Hope
'Neath mercy's cloak,
"The dark is almost light!"

Waken, Slumber!
Sleep not past
The painted dawn for thee.

Burst forth, O Star
One day not far
And shine Thy light on me.

—Beth Moore

To Amanda and Melissa

*When I was a child, I wanted to be a
"mommy" more than anything in the world.
Thank you for all the dreams you made come true.
I have no greater desire for your lives than
that you walk with God daily. He has been my passion.
May this and more be your heritage.*

*Love Beyond Expression,
Mom*

Introduction

I'm so humbled you've chosen to join me on a 10-week odyssey of prayer. No greater priority exists for the Believer than knowing Christ through the study of His Word and the intimacy of prayer. I am asking God to make you willing to commit to 70 days of consistent prayer. I estimate that most people will complete each day's format in 30 to 40 minutes. The time of day you choose to read your daily entry and write in your journal is up to you, but with all my heart I believe that this format will be most effective when used first thing in the morning.

These pages are offered to help you form a habit of prayer. If you miss a day or two, don't feel defeated and quit! Just get back to it as quickly as you can. I'm hoping the moments you spend in this journal will open the line of communication with God all day long. Remember, "Amen" doesn't mean "the end;" it means "So be it!"

In *Whispers of Hope*, you will find three features:

- Seventy Daily Devotionals—each complete with a brief Bible reading assignment, a Scripture for the day, and thoughts for the day.
- A Daily Prayer Guide: Following each devotional, you will find a prayer format for recording your petitions. Please thoroughly read instructions below entitled "Seventy Days of P.R.A.I.S.E." to understand the approach.
- Answer Log: Pages 254–258 are designated for answers to prayer. God is so faithful. Recording answers which seem to come quickly will help you be more patient as you wait on others. Recording answers will increase your awareness of God's goodness and fill your heart with gratitude.

Beloved, PRAYERFUL LIVES ARE POWERFUL LIVES! May God "teach us how to pray" (Luke 11:1) and may we be willing to learn! How deeply I pray that these pages will help you discover a fresh supply of mercy every morning, but more than that, may you discover the Mercy Giver.

Seventy Days of P.R.A.I.S.E.!
Sometimes a format can help us organize our thoughts—especially in a morning prayer time when we're just waking up! I am asking you to consider adopting the P.R.A.I.S.E. format for your prayer time during the next 10 weeks. The format will guide your journaling each day. I trust God to individualize how He desires to use this handbook in your personal life.

I'm certain of two things: prayerless lives are powerless lives, and prayerful lives are powerful lives. God will bestow riches beyond measure. Count on Him. Don't get caught up in trying to fill space on your prayer sheets! God will honor what you write from your heart. Enjoy God! May He become your delight!

For simple memorization, the following format is based on an acronym of the word PRAISE:

Praise: Begin your morning prayer time with praise. Psalm 22:3 tells us God inhabits the praises of His people. Sincere praise from your heart will invite God to pull up His chair and become your audience. You might repeat to Him a few of the attributes the Word records for Him. Tell Him Who He is! God already knows but He's wanting to make sure we know. Praising God helps remind us He is fully able to do anything we could ask or think according to His will. Tell Him how great He is and why you think so! You might repeat to Him the words to a hymn or worship chorus. Don't try to fit into a mold. Just praise Him with your heart.

Repentance: After you've spent several minutes in praise and worship, enter a time of confession and repentance. I teach this sequence because in Matthew 6:9,12 Christ taught the disciples to "hallow" God's name first, then ask for forgiveness for sin. However, I've experienced times when my heart was too full of sin and conviction to begin with praise. You probably have, too. Sometimes, based on Isaiah 59:1,2, you may need to begin your prayer time with repentance rather than praise. The Isaiah passage indicates that, when we have rebelled against God, all He wants to hear is repentance. David's prayer in Psalm 51 is an example. His life had been so full of sin, his prayer of repentance simply started with the words, "Have mercy upon me!" As you become increasingly sensitive to the Holy Spirit, you will discern times when your prayer life needs to begin with repentance rather than praise. Your heart will feel burdened with sin and anxious for relief. NO MATTER WHAT, practice a time of confession and repentance DAILY!! We gain victory over sin by allowing God to treat our problems in their earliest stages. Resist letting anything build up. Confess sins of the thought life such as wrong motives, negativism, a critical spirit, or even right words with a wrong heart. Let God catch things in early stages so we can be Spirit-filled people on a DAILY basis. Remember, the only thing whiter than snow is a freshly cleansed child of God! (Ps. 51:7).

Acknowledgment: Having praised Him and been purified by Him, you are ready to submit to God's authority. Acknowledge His right to rule and reign in your life everyday. Then willingly and DELIBERATELY submit yourself to His lordship—ONE DAY AT A TIME. Any day not surrendered to the authority of the Holy Spirit will automatically be lived in the flesh (see Gal. 5). Acknowledging God's specific authority over your personal life is not the same thing as praise. We can praise God all day long with our lips yet never deliberately surrender to His lordship with our hearts. Often in this part of my prayer time, I acknowledge how trustworthy He's been with His authority in my life. I recall how He has never misled me and that He calls upon me to submit to Him for MY SAKE... not for His. However you may word it, I urge you to make a specific point of acknowledging Him as Lord; voice your choice to bend your knee to Him. You might also ask Him for an immediate awareness when you are departing His authority. Acknowledge God's goodness to you in the past and thank Him for His faithfulness during times you've allowed Him to be the uncontested Lord of your life. This is a very important step. Please don't skip it!

Intercession: Pray for others! I'm overwhelmed by how many people need prayer. The list never ends! If you have a long prayer list, you might divide the list into days of the week. We probably pray more effectively over five or ten needs per day than fifty! Ask God to burden your heart with the specific people He wants you to intercede for each day. Intercessory prayer really works! Here's a tip: we save time when we don't tell God how to answer the prayer! God doesn't need our list of solutions. When Mary, Christ's mother, went to Christ with a petition in John 2:3, she simply stated the need. She knew He was God. Who could be more qualified to analyze the problem and apply the solution?

Supplication for self: Now enter into a time of prayer for yourself. I wholeheartedly disagree with both those who say we shouldn't pray for ourselves and those who make us feel selfish when we do. God has called each of us to love Him, serve Him, and live holy lives. I need help to live that life! We can only know Him intimately when we bring Him our innermost thoughts, fears, hurts, gains, losses and desires. This is a time when I just talk to Him. I ask Him to give me a heart to love Him more and to fill any empty or handicapped places in my heart with the safety of His love. I discuss with Him my tendencies and any weaknesses I'm experiencing. I share my needs and desires. I use this as a very personal time between the two of us. I hope you'll do the same. Pour out your heart to Him for God is our refuge (Ps. 62:8).

Equipping: Supplication for self helps us KNOW God; this step assists us as we grow in our capacity to SERVE God. Conclude your prayer time by asking Him to equip you in every way for a victorious day. You're cleansed and prepared for His full habitation, so ask Him to fill you with His Spirit, to make Himself "conspicuous" in you and to make you victorious over the evil one. Ask Him to give you eyes that "see" Him and ears sensitized to "hear" Him. Ask Him to give you a heart to respond when He opens a door of opportunity. Ask Him to empower you to witness as He leads! Invite Him to equip you with the power of the heavenlies—a double portion of the Holy Spirit. "How much more will your Father in heaven give the Holy Spirit to those who ask him!" ASK HIM FOR IT ALL! May God fold His everlasting arms around us one day in Glory and say, "This child withheld nothing from me."

What About Thanksgiving?

Philippians 4:6 says, "in everything, by prayer and petition, with thanksgiving, present your requests to God." Incorporate thanksgiving into every aspect of your prayer time. As you PRAISE, thank Him for choosing to reveal Himself to you. As you REPENT, thank Him for His faithfulness to forgive your sins. As you ACKNOWLEDGE His lordship, thank Him for being so trustworthy with His authority. As you INTERCEDE, thank Him for being your Great High Priest and adding power to your petitions. In SUPPLICATION for yourself, thank Him for knowing you intimately and desiring that you know Him. As you ask for EQUIPPING, thank Him for never calling on you to do anything He will not readily equip you to accomplish. In EVERYTHING, THANK HIM!

NICHOLAS PAVLOFF

Day One

"In the beginning God created the heavens and the earth....
And God saw that it was good" (Gen. 1:1,25).

Scripture Reading: Genesis 1:1-27; 2:1-3

God recorded His word through the pens of inspired men chiefly for one reason—to tell us about Himself. In the first few sweeps of ink, He demonstrated something vastly important among His attributes: He is CREATIVE. Scarcely before the ink could dry in the first sentence, God revealed something else—He is ORDERLY.

Only God could combine wholly creative and completely orderly. Some of us are refreshingly creative and others, thankfully, are orderly; but often we can hardly abide one another. If wisdom prevails, however, we eventually discover we need one another or our different contributions are unbalanced and lacking.

God, on the other hand, needed no one to complete Him. He created the heavens and the earth simply because He wanted to. Afterward, He looked on His perfect blend of creativity and orderliness and said, "This is good—very good in fact." God still considers a blend of creativity and order an effective way of working with us. If you are His child, God is working in your life in both creative and orderly ways. He desires to be entirely creative with you. Do you allow Him the freedom?

What God is doing in your life right now may not make sense to you, but it's not because He's nonsensical. It's because He's creative. God wants us to surrender to His will, but we tend to want a blueprint of His plans so we can decide whether or not to surrender. In John 21:21, after Christ gave Peter a glimpse of his future, Peter asked a question splitting at the seams with human nature: "Lord, what about him?" Like us, Peter derived a strange sense of security from sameness. As you search for your calling, do you attempt to find someone He is using in exactly the same way? Stop! Of the six billion people on this planet, that person may not exist—because God is creative.

Some can easily relate to the variety in God's plan. We thrive on creativity. Sameness bores us, but we still need the dependable security God offers. Creativity by itself creates only chaos. Our perfectly balanced God is also orderly. He has a day-by-day plan for your life. That's why it's so important to meet with Him—you guessed it—day by day.

Had you been a spectator during only the first three days of creation, you might not have judged it as good. What good are seed-bearing plants with no sun for photosynthesis? In His wisdom, God knew the work was good because He knew what was coming next. He knows what's coming next for you. That's why He can judge His work in you as good. Give God room to be completely creative. Meet with Him daily as He unfolds the plan in perfect order. He's really good at what He does.

Take a few moments to think of reasons to praise our creative and orderly God. Then lift those praises to Him in an attitude of thanksgiving.

Praise

....

....

....

....

....

....

Repentance

....

....

....

....

....

....

Acknowledgment

....

....

....

....

....

Intercession

....

....

....

....

....

....

Supplication for Self

....

....

....

....

....

....

Equipping

....

....

....

....

....

Day Two

"Do not gloat over me, my enemy! Though I have fallen, I will rise.
Though I sit in darkness, the Lord will be my light" (Mic. 7:8).

Scripture Reading: Micah 7:8-10

Sometimes our departures from God result from willful disobedience and premeditated sin—the wide-eyed sin we practically pencil in on our calendars. We've all experienced times when we knew we were about to do or say something that was willful, arrogant sin. We've all committed it and it's not pretty. "Falling" into sin develops from a different scenario. Although it equally misses the mark and requires the same repentance and forgiveness, falling into sin is not willful disobedience. In Micah 7:8, the word *fallen* comes from the Hebrew word *naphal*. The Hebrew lexicon states: "The main idea behind this root is a violent or accidental circumstance or event."[1]

I have a scar on my knee from falling over broken concrete while jogging one morning. I did not throw myself over the concrete on purpose; still the fall was my fault because I should have been watching where I was going. As I brushed off my hands and knees, I felt foolish and, frankly, was on the verge of tears. As the blood dripped into my sock, a passerby asked if she could take me home. I declined because I was too proud to let her. Ashamed, I hobbled my way home.

I've certainly committed premeditated sin, but I've also "fallen" into sin. I've been jogging along in my Christian life, become distracted with the scenery, believed I had things under control, stopped watching where I was going, and wham! Fallen into sin.

Falling into sin issues a unique invitation to the enemy. When we're involved in willful sin Satan only has to cheer us on, but when we "fall" he sows shame and "gloats" over us. He makes us feel foolish because we thought we were making progress. When we blow it, he constantly attempts to reinforce our worst fear: we're failures and we're never going to get it right. The shame is almost instantaneous.

When we fall, we must get up, allow God to immediately drive us home and bind up our wounds of foolishness. We must choose whether to play or to avoid the shame game. If we refuse to let the enemy gloat over us, our falls will become fewer and less violent. Our falls will become stumbles.

Is the memory of a bad fall still getting to you? Rather than allowing the enemy to continue to gloat over you, allow God to guide you. Have guts enough to say: "Do not gloat over me, my enemy! Though I have fallen, I will rise—stronger than ever, alert and watching."

Satan's mission is to trip us. I have a physical scar that reminds me every day of a spiritual reality. Please don't wait until you have a scar to learn the lesson. Don't take your eyes off the path—no matter how many times you've run that way before. Look to the One "who is able to keep you from falling" (Jude 24).

Praise

....

....

....

....

....

Repentance

....

....

....

....

Acknowledgment

....

....

....

....

Intercession

....

....

....

....

....

....

Supplication for Self

....

....

....

....

....

....

Equipping

....

....

....

....

....

....

J.D. MARSTON

Day Three

"Then they said, 'Come, let us build ourselves a city, with a tower that reaches to the heavens, so that we may make a name for ourselves and not be scattered over the face of the whole earth'" (Gen. 11:4).

Scripture Reading: Genesis 11:1-9

We humans struggle with the fear that God is trying to cheat us. God's command that we fill the earth with our offspring (Gen. 9:1) was a blessing—not a curse. God was wooing our ancestors to the spacious places He had created for them.

We humans again thought God was trying to cheat us when He made known His intention for us to glorify His name. We wanted our own name. The Tower of Babel was about humans making a name for ourselves. Our attempt to build "a tower that reaches to the heavens" was a means of planting our feet presumptuously on God's turf. We misunderstood—all creation is God's turf. I can almost imagine the Holy Trinity with drawn brow, intently watching our efforts to build the tower. Had our actions not been so galling and rebellious, the scene might have been comical.

God's response? "If they're this foolish and self-centered, they'll try anything."

Brick after brick, we humans sought to determine our own fate. Despite all the efforts, we never imposed our will on God, but God imposed His on us.

"Come, let us go down." The Father, Son, and Holy Spirit loaded up and headed down. What a scene. Imagine it! "The Lord scattered them...over all the earth." They experienced the world's first tumbling lesson.

Even today people rebel against God and insist on making a name for themselves. The many people who have attempted to climb Mount Everest provide a modern-day parable. They spend fortunes, suffer all manner of maladies, risk relationships, and endanger life and limb. They experience a level of cold no average person can imagine to trudge past frozen bodies. But do you know what mystifies me most? If they make it to the top, they can't even enjoy the thrill of victory. Their heads pound. They're disoriented. Their lungs nearly collapse. They suffer snow blindness. They stand on top of the famed Mt. Everest for five minutes and begin a hasty descent while they can still breathe. Why do they do it? For the sheer accomplishment of climbing to the highest peak on earth and the accompanying notoriety. Ironically, by the time they achieve the goal, most of them can't even remember their names.

Sounds rather like the Tower of Babel doesn't it? We humans want to make a name for ourselves. If we only understood that when we devote our lives to the glory of God, our existence on planet Earth will leave marks—eternal marks.

Those who reject God unify over one thing—every person's right to make a name for himself. They cheat themselves of the most glorious of all privileges: to bear the name of Jesus, the One and Only. And at His name...every knee shall bow.

Praise

....
....
....
....
....
....

Repentance

....
....
....
....
....

Acknowledgment

....
....
....
....
....

Intercession

....

....

....

....

....

Supplication for Self

....

....

....

....

....

Equipping

....

....

....

....

Day Four

"He sent forth his word and healed them; he rescued them from the grave"
(Ps. 107:20).

Scripture Reading: Psalm 107:10-21

The psalm does not reflect the ravages of and restoration from physical illness. In this text God sent His Word to heal a different illness—rebellion against God and refusal to accept His counsel. In their attempt to be free from His authority, God's people became prisoners in iron chains. Psalm 107:20 makes one of the most important statements about healing in all Scripture. God's Word is His primary healing agent. God's people were in bondage because they rebelled and refused His counsel. They were suffering because they lacked God's Word. Only His Word could heal them.

Many of us desperately need the healing power of God's Word. The Scripture is the written Word that reveals to us the living Word who is able to deliver us.

We sometimes act as if rebellion means drugs, a season of infidelity, or a complete apostasy. The biblical definition is simply refusing God's counsel. Isaiah 50:5 says, "The Sovereign Lord has opened my ears, and I have not been rebellious; I have not drawn back." Observe his words, "I have not been rebellious; I have not drawn back." Rebellion is drawing back from God's Word. We can attend church Sunday after Sunday and still rebel against God. If we continue to seek answers elsewhere and do not take God's Word seriously, we are in a state of rebellion.

I've experienced this kind of rebellion. In early adulthood my heart needed healing. I knew God. I served Him, but I ached for release—YET I never considered His Word as a cure for my illness. Fortunately, in my growing desire to please the Father, I realized I did not harbor a love for His Word. I began asking Him to develop such a love within me. As He did, something I never expected happened to me. My heart began to heal. I knew I was healthier. I felt it. I didn't begin studying God's Word so I could become whole, but I soon discovered that the more I sought His counsel, the more I healed. The process continues today, and I've gained far more than health. I've gained a deep love relationship with the Healer.

Please hear my heart. Healing is found in God's Word—not just in seeking healing—but in seeking Him. We can be children of the living God and still sit "in darkness and the deepest gloom" as "prisoners suffering in iron chains" because we refuse His counsel. The writer of Psalm 119:92 testified to the healing power of God's Word. "If your law had not been my delight, I would have perished in my affliction." Only God can set you free. His Word can soak the chains from your wrists.

Is there an area of your life that needs healing? Perhaps an undisciplined life, a festered wound, or a binding addiction? Write it down. Tell it to the Great Physician; then seek God's Word for healing.

Praise

....

....

....

....

....

....

Repentance

....

....

....

....

....

....

Acknowledgment

....

....

....

....

....

Intercession

....

....

....

....

....

Supplication for Self

....

....

....

....

....

Equipping

....

....

....

....

....

NICHOLAS PAVLOFF

Day Five

*"Therefore, I tell you, her many sins have been forgiven—for she loved much.
But he who has been forgiven little loves little" (Luke 7:47).*

Scripture Reading: Luke 7:36-50

Luke 7 invites us to dine at the table of contrast. We witness Christ in relation to two people, both equally loved by the One who sent His Son to dinner that night.

First we sit across from the Pharisee. Try to avoid stereotyping him. Many Pharisees were devoutly righteous men of God. Some were hypocrites, but others were genuine, striving desperately to keep the law. The Pharisee who invited Christ to dinner possessed volumes of scriptural knowledge. He could have recited literally hundreds of verses. He could have debated every Old Testament subject with intelligence and confidence. Let's give him the benefit of the doubt and assume he was a good man—and probably a curious man.

The host and his guest scarcely had time to greet each other and get comfortable before an intruder walked through the door. The host was appalled that a woman of the streets would enter his home. Imagine his embarrassment when the uninvited guest got down on her knees, wept at Christ's feet, and anointed them with perfume!

After delivering a mental verdict of "guilty" over her, the Pharisee placed Christ on the stand as well. He judged, "If this man were a prophet, he would know who is touching him and what kind of woman she is—that she is a sinner" (Luke 7:39).

I wonder if just once the Pharisee had ever used the term to describe himself. You see, to a man who had lived a righteous life, the word never applied to him—always to someone else. The Pharisee could not comprehend the sinful woman's actions because he could not comprehend the depth of her love. He had everything to offer Christ that evening: a spotless record, knowledge, stimulating conversation—but he had no love. She had nothing to offer Christ that evening but a terrible record. She was almost assuredly illiterate, and she couldn't talk for crying. But she had love.

We could interpret this encounter to mean the more we sin, the more we'll love Jesus. It seems to support depraved living as the key to deep loving. Not so! The woman's deep love did not flow from deep sin. It flowed from deep forgiveness. The level of intimacy her repentance required plummeted her to a depth of love. The Pharisee was also a sinner, but he was blinded by pride and strangled by self-righteousness.

God's mercy does not make sin tolerable; it makes sin forgivable. The proud and the depraved alike must kneel at the same feet for mercy. For those willing, God turns sin's empty cistern into a deep wellspring overflowing with love.

Do you have something in your life for which you feel God cannot forgive you? Perhaps you cannot forgive yourself. Open your heart to God's forgiving, redeeming love. He can forgive you—and He will—if you ask Him. His Word declares it.

Praise

....

....

....

....

....

Repentance

....

....

....

....

....

Acknowledgment

....

....

....

....

....

Intercession

....

....

....

....

....

....

Supplication for Self

....

....

....

....

....

....

Equipping

....

....

....

....

....

Day Six

"The words of a gossip are like choice morsels;
they go down to a man's inmost parts" (Prov. 26:22).

Scripture Reading: Proverbs 11:13; 16:28; 26:20-28

Most of us readily agree that gossip is wrong, yet we love it. We crave it. We nearly fall out of our chairs leaning to hear it. We spend fortunes on magazines that publish it. We know God wants us to avoid gossip, but it pulls us like wild horses pull a wagon. Let's identify a few of those wild horses. What drives us to gossip?

- *Boredom.* Nothing appeals to the senses like a soap opera. Our personal lives are often in a rut. We need a little excitement and someone else's life temporarily delivers.
- *Curiosity.* God created us to be curious so we would seek knowledge and grow. Listening to gossip is a counterfeit of the God-given desire for knowledge.
- *Jealousy.* We especially enjoy gossip if it concerns someone we envy. When we allow the flesh to control us, we are more likely to enjoy hearing that someone we envy looks worse than we do. The news may even make us feel better about ourselves.
- *Companionship.* Misery loves company. "Well, at least I'm not the only one whose family is in a mess!"
- *Importance.* We sometimes enjoy being considered a person in-the-know. We may attempt to impress others with how much we know.
- *Misdirected "concern."* Sometimes we share confidential information in the name of "concern." We all have experienced, perhaps even participated in, situations where gossip was dressed up with a hat and gloves and called a "prayer request."

Review the list of drives that fuel gossip. Determine which is the most and the least powerful in your life. Reflect on the settings where you are most tempted to gossip. Stop right now and ask God to forgive you for the times you've gossiped and to keep you alert to possible gossip traps.

We've all been guilty of gossip, but what do we do about such a driven team of tongues? We can let God tame those wild horses! He can rope the horse gone wild.

- *Boredom* can be remolded into a passion for Christ.
- *Curiosity* can drive us to know Christ.
- Transformed *jealousy* can fuel a passion "for" others' highest good.
- Our quest for miserable *companionship* can become our expression of mercy.
- Craving *importance* can push us to learn our true identity in Christ.
- *Misdirected "concern"* can become compassion tempered with discretion.

Does it sound too idealistic to try? Don't believe the enemy's lies! Ask God which of these are driving you to gossip and allow Him to tame them.

The next time you are tempted to repeat something you've heard to an eager listener, share a blessing from God instead. Rope 'em...tame 'em...and "move 'em out."

Praise

....

....

....

....

....

....

Repentance

....

....

....

....

....

Acknowledgment

....

....

....

....

....

Intercession

....

....

....

....

....

....

Supplication for Self

....

....

....

....

....

....

Equipping

....

....

....

....

....

NICHOLAS PAVLOFF

Day Seven

*"You also, like living stones, are being built into a spiritual house
to be a holy priesthood offering spiritual sacrifices
acceptable to God through Jesus Christ" (1 Pet. 2:5).*

Scripture Reading: 1 Peter 2:4-6

Under the inspiration of the Spirit, Peter called believers in Christ "living stones." The New Testament contains several different Greek words for *rock*. Christ referred to Peter as the *petros* or "piece of a rock" in Matthew 16:18,[2] but Peter referred to believers with a different word. He used *lithos,* which can refer to small or large stones.[3] Interestingly, *lithos* is also the original term used for the stone rolled away from Christ's tomb. Wouldn't it be something if our lives became living stones exposing the empty tomb—the proof Jesus lives? What if people were convinced we worship a living Savior simply by watching the effervescent life of the Spirit in us?

Most unbelievers still confuse Christianity and "religion." They charge us with walking on crutches of ancient rituals and laws. They have no interest in becoming what they observe us to be: walking mummies, bound in tight bandages of lifeless religion. We are people of eternal life—but they often see us as the earthly dead.

One of the primary reasons God leaves us on earth after we receive the Savior is to demonstrate flesh-and-blood proof that Christ lives. We are set-apart from dead religion because we have a living Redeemer. As living stones, do our lives expose an empty tomb and a living, thriving, personal God? Are we proof Christ lives? Do people walk into our churches and see us as living stones gathered in a spiritual house? If so, we'll never have to beg for visitors. People are desperately searching for signs of life. They will practically beat down our church doors if rumors of life erupt. Eternal "life" doesn't begin when we die. It began the moment we were reborn.

To really live we need passion for Jesus and purpose to serve Him. Passion and purpose fulfill more of our human needs than health or wealth. Plenty of healthy and wealthy people feel dead, meaningless, and hopeless. We represent hope to people who may have given up on finding real life. We are stones rolled away, giving them a glance into the empty tomb. We provide evidence that Jesus is the Resurrection and the Life. Do yourself and your neighbors a great big favor. Don't wait for death to really live. Tell God you want to be a neon sign of life—lingering proof of the resurrection. For "as Christ was raised up from the dead by the glory of the Father, even so we also should walk in newness of life" (Rom. 6:4, KJV).

How can you show proof of a living Savior to non-Christian friends and loved ones? Do you have a friend who needs to see Christ living and active in your life? Share what God is doing in your life and commit to be a living stone before your friend.

Get rolling, Living Stone, and show a little proof!

Praise

....

....

....

....

....

....

Repentance

....

....

....

....

....

Acknowledgment

....

....

....

....

....

Intercession

....

....

....

....

....

Supplication for Self

....

....

....

....

....

Equipping

....

....

....

....

....

Day Eight

*"If we confess our sins, he is faithful and just and will forgive us our sins
and purify us from all unrighteousness" (1 John 1:9).*

Scripture Reading: 1 John 1:5-10

One day when the accuser was busily doing His job in my life over a past sin, I claimed 1 John 1:9 out loud. Suddenly the Holy Spirit highlighted a word that had missed my attention in the past. The word was *just*.

New Testament *forgiveness* means "to let go free, let escape."[4] Is God willing to let a sinner escape? I know God's willingness to forgive my sins is an act of His faithfulness, but how could it also be an act of His justice? For justice to be truly served, don't I deserve to pay for my sins like prisoners pay for their crimes?

Take a look at the meaning of the word *just*. *Dikaios* means "that one conforms in his actions to his constitutionally just character. The rules are self-imposed." Justice is a standard no human can meet. No person can by his or her behavior fully meet the expectations of God (see Rom. 3:10).[5] Without the cross of Christ, forgiveness and justice cannot coexist. We would be hopeless; our confession of sin could bring only a "just" verdict: guilty—and a swift sentence: death.

Christ came to earth and became a man with the purpose of meeting all of God's expectations. He pleased the Father in every way. Then Jesus had to "become" every possible sin so justice could be served for the unjust. "God made him who had no sin to be sin" (2 Cor. 5:21). The guilty verdict came down; the sentence was passed. At Calvary God "self-imposed" a rule that has never been broken: all who accept the offer of God's blessed "stand-in" instantaneously have justice served for every sin they commit and find relief for every sin they confess.

Every time we confess our sins, He is not only faithful to forgive us, but He is also just. He sticks with His own self-imposed rule. He looks back on the cross, remembers the penalty paid, and "conforms in his actions to his constitutionally just character."[6]

Here lies one of the most important elements of God's self-imposed rule of justice served on sin: He is not bound by legalism just because of the cross. If He desired, our Savior could still crack open the floor of the earth and consume us. God can break the rules because He makes the rules! He is bound by love because of the cross. Compelled by unfathomable love for His Son and the sons of men, He has obligated Himself. At this point the "faithfulness" in 1 John 1:9 enters in: He will never change. His character is spotless. He made a promise He will never break no matter what depth of sin we may confess. His faithfulness is not out of duty because nothing can force God's hand. His faithfulness is a binding covenant of choice.

Child of God, you need not be afraid. "If we confess our sins, he is faithful and just and will forgive us our sins and purify us from all unrighteousness" (1 John 1:9).

Praise

....

....

....

....

....

....

Repentance

....

....

....

....

....

Acknowledgment

....

....

....

....

....

Intercession

....
....
....
....
....
....

Supplication for Self

....
....
....
....
....
....

Equipping

....
....
....
....
....
....

NICHOLAS PAVLOFF

Day Nine

"Whatever you do, do it all for the glory of God" (1 Cor. 10:31).

Scripture Reading: 1 Corinthians 10:14-33

In two short phrases, the apostle Paul practically wrote a thesis on simplification. For every one of us who ever wondered where to draw the line, juggled too many balls at once, or had trouble making up our mind, Paul offers a timely simplification: "Whatever you do, do it all for the glory of God." We differ in talents, gifts, and resources, but the hands of time strangle us all. We desperately need a time management course—but who can fit it in?

When our beloved Michael was little, he loved to "help" me grocery shop. Once he begged me to buy our dogs a large bag of rawhide bones. His face was so animated that I agreed, but when we arrived home I forgot about the purchase. Michael—always quite a sneak—slipped the bag out without my noticing. Later that day a strange commotion in the backyard seized my attention. Our dog, Sunny, was hopping frantically in every direction, kicking up more grass than a weed eater, and panting as if she were fighting for her last few breaths. When I walked out to investigate, I heard Michael laughing mischievously, and then I saw them—at least a hundred "bones" scattered all over the backyard. Sunny was frenzied. So little time—so many bones!

Don't get me wrong. I'm not "dogging" us for trying. Most of our "bones" are good ones. We've just got too many to chew. In our attempt to do a hundred good things, we may not do any of them well. We're caught in the captivity of activity—hopping frantically in every direction, tongues dragging and lungs panting. We're dog tired.

God never meant for us to live frenzied lives. Backbreaking schedules are not His idea. How can we, believers in Christ, restructure our lives and find a little refreshment?

- **Reestablish the goal.** Isaiah 43:7 tells us we were created for His glory. The purpose of our brief journey on this planet is to glorify God. He desires for us to pour the best of our energies into God works. Go back to the basics.
- **Redirect your focus.** Matthew 6:33 makes a revolutionary promise. If we seek God first, He will direct our schedules and help us to discern His priorities through the work of the Holy Spirit. Give the Matthew 6:33 approach a try! It really works!
- **Rethink your motivation.** Galatians 1:10 prompts us to ask ourselves if any of our activities are seeking man's approval rather than God's. If we seek to please people rather than God, rules will constantly change and expectations will soar.
- **Rest in God's will.** Hebrews 4:10 says, "Anyone who enters God's rest also rests from his own work."

Sounds wonderful, doesn't it? God is not unreasonable. He does not heap on stress and then refuse to grant us rest. None of us can do one hundred things to the glory of God. Let's find rest in His will and do a few things well.

Praise

....

....

....

....

....

Repentance

....

....

....

....

....

Acknowledgment

....

....

....

....

....

Intercession

....

....

....

....

....

Supplication for Self

....

....

....

....

....

Equipping

....

....

....

....

....

Day Ten

"I led them with cords of human kindness, with ties of love" (Hos. 11:4).

Scripture Reading: Hosea 11:1-4; Joel 2:18-32

Thousands of years ago, God made a covenant with a wanderer named Abram to raise up a nation through which He would bring the Savior of the world. In Hosea 11:1-4, God talks about that nation. He describes Israel as a child He nurtured and taught to walk. God describes the countless ups and downs with His "child" and how when she rebelled against Him or rejected His love, God remained faithful to His covenant. He made promises to this child and He honored His Word.

Although at times Israel was unfaithful, God was faithful. Why?

The answer is hidden in Deuteronomy 7:6-8: "The Lord your God has chosen you out of all the peoples on the face of the earth to be his people, his treasured possession. The Lord did not set his affection on you and choose you because you were more numerous than other peoples, for you were the fewest of all peoples. But it was because the Lord loved you and kept the oath he swore to your forefathers." God is faithful to His people because He loves.

Of all God's wonders, I am perhaps most astonished by His stubborn love. Through the long roller-coaster ride of history, God continued to love Israel—and He will continue to love us.

Our obedience on this earth directly influences blessing and reward, but it has nothing to do with His love. He cannot look at you apart from His love. He cannot hear your pleas for mercy with anything but a Father's ear. He is incapable of being unbiased toward you. He cannot momentarily resign His position as your Father to make an impartial decision. He's committed, no matter what.

You cannot explain nor comprehend God's persistent love. It's just how He is. You are His child. 1 John 4:16 says, "And so we know and rely on the love God has for us." We can't "rely" on something we have never accepted. God's love for us is lavish (see 1 John 3:1). By the time we were knit in our mothers' wombs, our lives were like open books before Him—every sentence read, every paragraph indented, every chapter titled, every page numbered. He knew it all in advance—all the sin, all the selfishness, every weakness. Yet He chose to love us—lavishly. Sometimes God allows us to reach a point where we realize we can rely on absolutely nothing—except His love.

Perhaps you are one who thinks that God shouldn't be bothered with the little things you can handle alone. Have you faced a circumstance over which you had no control? Do you remember the relief and release you felt when you lifted that burden to Him?

God is willing to take every burden, every day, even the ones we think we can fix in our own strength. He will give us that relief and release daily. Try it—right now.

Praise

....

....

....

....

....

....

Repentance

....

....

....

....

....

Acknowledgment

....

....

....

....

....

Intercession

....

....

....

....

....

....

Supplication for Self

....

....

....

....

....

Equipping

....

....

....

....

....

NICHOLAS PAVLOFF

Day Eleven

"In the same way, the Spirit helps us in our weakness. We do not know what we ought to pray for, but the Spirit himself intercedes for us with groans that words cannot express" (Rom. 8:26).

Scripture Reading: Romans 8:19-27

These verses are about groanings. Three kinds, in fact. First, creation groans for the return of Christ and His saints. Subject to the frustration of being created by Him and for Him, yet absent from Him, all creation longs to be liberated from its innate corrosion and made new in the presence of its Creator.

Secondly, we groan inwardly as we eagerly await our adoption. Those of us in Christ recognize this groaning whether or not we've ever identified it. When did you last feel weary of the pain of this world? Perhaps not your sufferings, but another's? Hungry children on the other side of the world. Hospitals filled with the dying. Violence and hatred. We groan. We just don't recognize the source of the ache—to be safe and sound in our new home, nestled in the down comforter of Christ's love. We are no longer orphaned. Yet neither are we home. As pleasant as our foster homes here on earth may be, we never cease to be startled by the world's meanness. Our groanings bring voice to feelings we often can't identify: "Rescue us, O Savior!"

The passage identifies a third type of groaning—the groaning of the Spirit of God as He intercedes for us. Sometimes we can better discern the meaning of a Scripture passage by identifying what it clearly does not mean. Romans 8:26 does not say the Holy Spirit will intercede for us when we are too busy to pray, too angry to pray, too involved in ministry to pray, or too disappointed in God to pray. The passage says the Spirit intercedes for us when we are too weak to know how to pray. He intercedes not because we simply don't pray—but when we don't know *how* to pray.

Imagine this poignant scene. The child of God musters her last bit of strength to collapse before the throne of God. Words do not come—just groanings. They are not her groanings, though they emerge from so deep within, she thinks they are hers. The Spirit of God searches her heart, gathers her pain, and lifts it to the Father of all comfort. The Spirit of God, knowing both the depth of her agony and the will of the Father, can bring forth glory from even this. He insists that the Father usher overflowing comfort. He urges the child to let the Father have His way. He prays for things she could not bear to pray—that she lacks the courage to pray. He prays for glory.

How long does the child lay before God's throne? Until strength comes. Until she identifies the heart of the Spirit's intercession for her and can make it her own. Perhaps this is one of life's finest hours for the believer—when the will of the Father and the will of the child converge as one—and the cloudy pillar of God's glory settles on her shoulders like a down comforter. And for just a moment, heaven comes to earth.

Praise

....

....

....

....

....

....

Repentance

....

....

....

....

....

....

Acknowledgment

....

....

....

....

....

Intercession

....

....

....

....

....

Supplication for Self

....

....

....

....

Equipping

....

....

....

....

Day Twelve

"Examine yourselves to see whether you are in the faith;
test yourselves" (2 Cor. 13:5).

Scripture Reading: 2 Corinthians 13:1-10

Many believers struggle with assurance of their salvation. Because we've been called to lives of faith, Satan seizes every opportunity to sow doubt. Inspired by the Spirit, Paul exhorts us to "examine" and "test" ourselves to see whether we are in the faith. His next statement holds the key: "Do you not realize that Christ Jesus is in you—unless, of course, you fail the test?" (2 Cor. 13:5). Romans 8:9 tells us, "If anyone does not have the Spirit of Christ, he does not belong to Christ." We should "examine" ourselves for earmarks of Christ's presence. His Spirit is so totally alien to ours, we can quickly observe the difference if we're willing to put ourselves to the test.

Look back at Paul's question once more: "Do you not realize that Christ Jesus is in you?" We can paraphrase his question: "Do you not see realities that Christ Jesus is in you?" Christ's presence within us creates realities completely foreign to us. His inner dwelling is obvious in several remarkable ways. Let's note just a few:

1) *Conviction of sin.* Without Christ, we lack a supernatural sorrow over sin. We may feel guilty, but human guilt differs from the conviction experienced by the redeemed. Guilt centers on ourselves and others. Conviction is the realization that our sin personally offends God. When convicted, our wrongdoing is a God issue rather than merely a people issue. Remember, Christ's Spirit is "holy," so He reacts to anything unholy. The Spirit is the One causing us to squirm. In our humanity, we are not innately "good" enough to squirm over sin.

2) *A war with our old natures.* The Holy Spirit's task is to make us more like Christ. He takes up residence with a primary job: conformation. We may resist change—but when we do, we will sense the war within. In our natural selves we are not compelled to change, but our inner selves have compulsions to change.

3) *A strange sense of peace.* Even when we don't necessarily like God's choices for us, we experience a supernatural sense of inner peace when we submit and trust.

4) *An alien ability to respond like Christ.* When yielded to God's control, at times we will respond with feelings, words, or actions totally distinct from our own natures. We may sometimes think, *That couldn't have been me.* If we do not possess the Spirit of Christ, no matter how hard we attempt to "yield" to God's control, we will not experience that alien ability in our feelings and responses. We will be capable of "good works" but not "God works." Only a believer perceives the difference.

Remember, God doesn't think, speak, or act like us. Sudden displays of His character coming from within us are proof of our salvation. If we can examine ourselves and discover Christ, beloved, we are "in the faith!" Rest "assured."

Praise

....

....

....

....

....

....

Repentance

....

....

....

....

....

....

Acknowledgment

....

....

....

....

....

Intercession

....

....

....

....

....

....

Supplication for Self

....

....

....

....

....

Equipping

....

....

....

....

....

NICHOLAS PAVLOFF

Day Thirteen

*"Three times a day he got down on his knees and prayed, giving thanks
to his God, just as he had done before" (Dan. 6:10).*

Scripture Reading: Daniel 6

We're tempted to think of heroes like Daniel as supermen with powers unattainable to the average Joe. We cheat Daniel when we don't picture him as he was: a fragile man of flesh and blood, prone to run, and tempted to conform—just like the rest of us. But Daniel didn't run, even when faced with hungry lions licking off his flesh before doing the favor of killing him. What gave Daniel his courage? How did he maintain his integrity in matters of life and death? I think Daniel 6 reveals a few answers.

1) Daniel was already in the HABIT of prayer. Look at verse 10: He prayed "just as he had done before." He didn't just dial 911 in emergencies or 1411 for more information. He was in the habit of walking with God daily. I want my voice to be one God is accustomed to hearing every day. I don't want only a crisis relationship. I don't think you do, either. We derive tremendous security from knowing that the same God who met our needs yesterday will meet them today.

2) Daniel trusted in the sovereignty of God. Verse 10 says "he got down on his knees." He submitted himself to God's authority, trusting Him to override anything contrary to His will. I've tried to instill in my children the once-a-day habit of getting down on their knees to pray. The physical posture of bending the knee to God's authority reminds us He is Lord. This practice doesn't degrade me; it gives me great security.

3) Daniel cast himself entirely upon God. The word *prayed* in verse 10 translates a Hebrew word rarely used in Scripture. It means "to limp as if one-sided."[7] In his own strength, Daniel knew he was too handicapped to walk the path before him. Through prayer He cast his weight on God and took one step at a time.

4) Daniel unashamedly asked God for help. I believe he was scared to death. He had no intention of turning his back on God, but he was understandably frightened of the impending sentence. My favorite part of the story is that Daniel didn't receive the sort of help he anticipated. He probably asked for the edict to be overturned or for God to change King Darius' decision. Maybe he simply asked for courage to die with dignity for the glory of God. I doubt that he specifically asked God to shut the lions' mouths. But God showed that it wasn't Daniel's courage, King Darius' change of heart, or the group's guilty conscience that saved him. It was God. He doesn't always provide the sort of help we anticipate—but His method always provokes the most glory.

Beloved, we're living in the lions' den. Victory is ours when we walk with God daily in habitual prayer, when we know His Word well enough to trust His sovereignty, and when we cast ourselves on Him and make an honest plea for help. He derives great satisfaction from shutting that lion's mouth.

Praise

....

....

....

....

....

....

Repentance

....

....

....

....

....

Acknowledgment

....

....

....

....

....

Intercession

....

....

....

....

....

....

Supplication for Self

....

....

....

....

....

....

Equipping

....

....

....

....

....

Day Fourteen

"'Like clay in the hand of the potter, so are you in my hand,
O house of Israel'" (Jer. 18:6).

Scripture Reading: Jeremiah 18:1-12

Throughout Scripture God assumed the role of teacher. Like most effective instructors, He utilized a host of different methods. He based His teaching on a lesson plan primarily consisting of two sovereign words: *whatever works.*

In Exodus 31, God wrote His lesson on a chalkboard. (Then, of course, there was that unfortunate incident when His star pupil threw down the chalkboard and God had to write it again.)

In the Gospels, sometimes He gathered His class on the shore and taught them from a boat. (Great method if your students aren't too easily distracted.)

In Jeremiah 18, however, God used one of my personal favorites: He scheduled a field trip. He sent Jeremiah, one of His front-row students, to a potter's house without a clue what he would learn. When Jeremiah reached his destination, he saw the potter working at the wheel. The willing student watched over the potter's shoulder for quite some time (it doesn't say how long he watched, does it?) before God spoke.

The artist carefully shaped the pot; then Jeremiah saw it marred in the potter's hands. The artist took the same piece of clay and molded it into the shape of his own choosing. The work of a potter demands such attention that the workman may have been oblivious to Jeremiah's presence. Finally, God spoke: "'O house of Israel, can I not do with you as this potter does?...Like clay in the hand of the potter, so are you in my hand'" (Jer. 18:6).

As the Divine Potter, God introduced Himself vividly to the children of Israel as the God of second chances—the One who could take the marred, broken lump of clay and reshape it into something beautiful and useful. He would willingly turn His chastisements from them and write a new lesson plan—if they would let Him. He knew in advance what His people would do. They would consider the prospect, try to imagine themselves beautifully remade, count the cost and reply, "It's no use."

Can you imagine becoming a newly formed vessel in God's hands? A sacred and useful vessel? Have parts of you been marred for so long that you can't imagine how He could ever reshape you? Does the process seem too lengthy? Does it require too much cooperation? Do you sometimes think, *It's no use?* Sometimes we can see folly in others that we cannot see in ourselves. Didn't we wonder how Israel could have made such a poor choice when they were given another chance? How could they have been such cracked pots? To say "It's no use" is to say the Potter is not qualified to do what He does best. Take your chances on God. Put your life in His hands. Newness doesn't come from faith in yourself. It comes from faith in Him.

Praise

....

....

....

....

....

Repentance

....

....

....

....

....

Acknowledgment

....

....

....

....

....

Intercession

....

....

....

....

....

....

Supplication for Self

....

....

....

....

....

Equipping

....

....

....

....

....

NICHOLAS PAVLOFF

Day Fifteen

"Show me your ways, O Lord, teach me your paths" (Ps. 25:4).

Scripture Reading: Psalm 25:1-10

In her book, *Through Gates of Splendor,* Elizabeth Elliot tells the story of five young men who, compelled by the insurmountable love of Christ, offered their lives to free a savage people in the jungles of Ecuador. In January 1956, the five New Tribes missionaries ventured to share Christ with the feared Auca Indians. All five were killed in a savage encounter, but their blood became the seed out of which God raised new children for Himself. One life at a time, the Auca church was born and now bulges with believers whose testimonies are more dramatic than fiction.

Two of the same men who threw the deadly spears in 1956 later baptized the son of Nate Saint, one of the five martyred missionaries. In the late 1990s, the missionary's son and his family moved among the believing Aucas and continued the legacy left by five men who were "faithful unto death."

The Aucas testify to the faithfulness of Christ in ways indigenous to their culture. For generations they branded paths in the thick jungles by carving a mark on each side of the trees. Others would be able to find their way by following the carvings. Now they speak of the carvings left by Christ and His Word which mark "reliable paths." Scriptures in their language are written on boards and hung in their churches. They utilize these Scripture carvings to teach one another and their children to follow God's Word as "reliable paths."

They claim to have learned much from their once unwelcome visitors, but we have much to learn from them. They have allowed the gospel to radically change their lives. The practices of their people relentlessly handed down through the generations have been completely altered by the Word of God. Christ's gospel was a full-scale intrusion into their lives, yet when they chose Him, they chose His lifestyle…as unnatural as it was. They have followed His carvings to freedom.

Beloved, He has a reliable path for us as well. He knows exactly what He wants us to do in our present situations. The dilemma is weighing our genuine need for God's direction against our personal resistance to alteration.

The Auca's example of faith invites us to adopt the prayer of the psalmist who also searched for the "carvings" of God to lead him in perilous journeys: "Show me your ways, O Lord, teach me your paths." We encounter God's challenge as He demands: *Will you allow Me to dramatically alter your ways to teach you My own?*

Praise

....

....

....

....

....

....

Repentance

....

....

....

....

....

Acknowledgment

....

....

....

....

....

Intercession

....

....

....

....

....

....

Supplication for Self

....

....

....

....

....

Equipping

....

....

....

....

....

Day Sixteen

"Stop doing wrong, learn to do right!" (Isa. 1:16,17).

Scripture Reading: Isaiah 1:16,17 and Psalm 34:11-17

Far be it from me to divulge which one, but teaching one of my daughters to drive a car was a hair-raising experience. From the first moment she slid behind the wheel, she applied her highly spirited personality to the gas pedal.

Her no-nonsense philosophy at stop signs could only be described as "tap and go"—whether you're next in line or a Mack truck was coming. Her confusion over turn signals was somewhat disconcerting to fellow drivers. But most notable was the way she took a corner. I do mean she "took" the corner—practically mailbox and all—at full throttle. I've never known anyone else talented enough to remain tightly bound to the right-hand lane while taking a sharp corner at 30 miles per hour.

I finally screamed, "Repeat after me: THE BRAKE IS YOUR FRIEND!" Typical of our family brand of humor, we both laughed until our sides were splitting. Then in a serious parent-to-child tone I warned, "If you don't learn to use your brakes properly, Child, you're going to get yourself and a few others in a heap of trouble."

Our text today reflects a strong parent-to-child tone. In the first chapter of Isaiah, God addresses Israel as a child. He lays it on the line in verses 17 and 18: "Stop doing wrong, learn to do right!" Sometimes no other words will do. We can attempt to justify our tendencies to commit certain behaviors. We can retrace how we got ourselves in such a mess, but sometimes the Heavenly Father's simple and stern instruction is the only method that works: "Stop this now!" Then get on track and learn to do right.

One of the wisest and most necessary principles for a student driver in the faith is "Learn to apply the brakes." In other words, learn when to stop. In the middle of a collision is NOT the best time to learn how to use the brakes. Ideally, applying the brakes before the stop sign is the safest way to drive. When we are headed for trouble, the Holy Spirit will raise caution lights and stop signs. Sometimes He tells us to slow down, and sometimes He tells us to "STOP!" Surely we each remember a time when we wish we had applied the brakes when we first observed the signs. Hopefully, we learned from those painful collisions and now have a much better safety record. If we haven't had a wreck in awhile, we probably can look back and recall when we finally agreed to "stop doing wrong" and "learn to do right." Others of us may still be fishtailing in the middle of a dangerous intersection. God's Word cries out today: STOP! Put on the brakes before it's too late.

You may think I'm taking undue "license" with this lesson, but it's never too late to practice safe driving on life's rough road. Along the way we'll meet folks under the influence—the wrong influence. Be prepared. Listen to the Father when He says, "Repeat after me: THE BRAKE IS YOUR FRIEND!"

Praise

....

....

....

....

....

Repentance

....

....

....

....

....

Acknowledgment

....

....

....

....

Intercession

....

....

....

....

....

Supplication for Self

....

....

....

....

....

Equipping

....

....

....

....

....

NICHOLAS PAVLOFF

Day Seventeen

"Give me neither poverty nor riches, but give me only my daily bread. Otherwise, I may have too much and disown you and say, 'Who is the Lord?' or I may become poor and steal, and so dishonor the name of my God" (Prov. 30:8,9).

Scripture Reading: Proverbs 30:7-9

Heaven won't be paradise only because of what is present. It will also be paradise because of what is absent. Our future dwelling promises a list of "no mores," like no more tears, sorrow, or pain. One of my favorite "no mores," however, isn't in the Book of Revelation. You can count on it anyway, because we will have "no more" need of it, praise to our God! In heaven there will be no more money!

Aren't you tired of struggling with finances? Don't you sometimes think you'll have a throw-down fit if you receive another bill? Money. We love it. We hate it. We need it. We crave it. Nothing drives us crazy like money. Yet we can't get enough of it. When asked how much money is enough, a very wealthy man answered, "a little bit more." He spoke for all of us, didn't he? A rare soul admits he has enough.

Of course, having money isn't the real problem. Money having us is the issue. Our Scriptures for today explain how to "balance" our checkbooks. If you're like me, you probably could use a little help. Those illegible numbers we wrote on the back of our checkbooks made perfect sense when we scratched them there, didn't they? Actually, God's method of balancing our checkbooks isn't primarily about numbers. It's about attitude. Two reminders help us stay balanced in matters of money.

God's definition of the ideal salary is income that falls between the extremes of poverty and riches. If you don't have to steal to eat, you're not too poor. If you don't have a tendency to forget God, you're not too rich. I dare say most of us fall between the two extremes in Proverbs 30:8,9. You see, God views most of our financial situations as ideal because we aren't lacking in the necessities of life, yet we are still forced to depend on Him. I'm sure most of us would like to be among those put to the test of faithfulness with great riches, but we might be getting more than we bargained for. Money has a way of ignoring authority. Matthew 6:24 tells us, "You cannot serve both God and money." King David offered very wise advice when he said, "though your riches increase, do not set your heart on them" (Ps. 62:10). They are fleeting indeed.

God's tenure as head of the Department of Treasury: Psalm 24:1 says, "The earth is the Lord's, and everything in it, the world, and all who live in it." Every piece of gold and silver, every precious stone on this planet belongs to the Lord. All we have is His. He distributes it as He sees fit and attaches to it both blessings and testing.

Today's truths may seem simplistic, but if we adopt a more "balanced" approach to our finances, the noose of economic anxiety around our necks will loosen considerably. God is the Banker. Allow Him to balance your checkbook frequently.

Praise

....
....
....
....
....
....

Repentance

....
....
....
....
....

Acknowledgment

....
....
....
....
....

Intercession

....

....

....

....

....

Supplication for Self

....

....

....

....

....

Equipping

....

....

....

....

Day Eighteen

"That which was from the beginning, which we have heard, which we have seen with our eyes, which we have looked at and our hands have touched— this we proclaim concerning the Word of life" (1 John 1:1).

Scripture Reading: 1 John 1:1-4

I once had a well-meaning Sunday School teacher who made the statement, "If when life is over I discover I was wrong in what I believed, at least I will have lived the good life." We all nodded nobly. I remember thinking: *I guess he's right. Even if we're wrong, we've lived good, honest lives and helped people.* The more I grew in God's Word, however, the more I considered the philosophy outrageous. We have not made up a "religion," been misled by emotions, or concocted answers in our desperation.

The Spirit birthed the church in the hearts of eyewitnesses—people who saw Christ with their own eyes and touched Him with their own hands. John watched as Jesus was transfigured on the mountain. He saw Christ raise the dead. He heard Jesus foretell His suffering and death on the cross; then he watched in horror at the fulfillment of every detail. He saw Mary Magdalene's expression when she came with the news of the empty tomb. He ran to see the evidence for himself. Later John gathered with the other disciples behind locked doors when Christ appeared among them. He saw Christ's pierced hands and side with his own eyes.

The twelve were not the only ones who saw the resurrected Christ with their own eyes. 1 Corinthians 15:6 tells us Christ appeared to 500 other followers assembled in one place. By the time Christ gathered with His disciples to commission them, He had erased all doubt. He said, "And you will be my witnesses" (Acts 1:8). Eyewitnesses. They watched their risen Savior ascend into the heavens, then lived the rest of their days on the passionate certainty of what they had seen...and touched. These followers did not lay down their lives for their hopes. Facing the sword has a strange way of sobering a soul. Honesty surfaces and nobility disappears. Had they doubted, at least one of them would have broken under the pressure to save his own skin. Not one of them withheld a single moment of their lives from Christ. The same 12 men who once struggled with pride, disbelief, and inability were transformed into unstoppable powerhouses, undaunted by imprisonment, persecution, and the threat of death.

Beloved, the New Testament church was birthed on facts—not myths, legends, or well-meaning philosophies, but on things seen, heard, touched, and experienced. Things the twelve could not keep to themselves. They didn't just believe. They knew! In those uneasy moments when you realize how outnumbered you are and how many people do not believe, remember: our faith is founded on fact. When life is over, you will not have simply lived the good life...you will see with your eyes and touch with your hands the Way, the Truth, and the Life.

Praise

....

....

....

....

....

....

Repentance

....

....

....

....

....

Acknowledgment

....

....

....

....

....

Intercession

....

....

....

....

....

....

Supplication for Self

....

....

....

....

....

....

Equipping

....

....

....

....

....

NICHOLAS PAVLOFF

Day Nineteen

"Delight yourself in the Lord and he will give you the desires of your heart" (Ps. 37:4).

Scripture Reading: Psalm 37:1-24

God knows us so well. In His infinite wisdom, He knew that even noble, believing humans would attempt to use Him as a means of getting ahead. Our motive for seeking God is often self-centered. Ideally, He enjoys being sought for the pleasure of His presence. He then delights in allowing the seeker to discover wonderful gains, but, because He knows us so well, He has methods for making the most of our sometimes questionable motives. He allows our greed to lead us on a treasure hunt where we ultimately discover the greatest treasure of all.

Psalm 37:4 is a perfect example—a feel-good Scripture if ever you'll find one. God knew we would seek a Scripture promising the desires of our hearts. He also knew our self-seeking search could lead us to an incomparable treasure. The end result motivates our first approach to Psalm 37:4: "He will give you the desires of your heart." Then the "end" causes us to consider the means: "Delight yourself in the Lord." True to our human form we become attentive to the means so we can reach the end.

We begin to question, "How can I delight myself in the Lord?" We can almost hear Him whisper, "I'm so glad you asked." As we make ourselves available to delight in God, He slowly revolutionizes our approach to finding fulfillment. Those who seek to delight in the Lord will ultimately develop a delightful relationship with Him; however, by the time God makes Himself the seeker's delight, the once self-seeking treasure hunter has been transformed.

Anyone who truly delights in the Lord will one day realize that God has become the desire of her heart. When He is our delight, we begin to want what He wants. We come to trust His best for us. When we struggle with self-seeking desires, we hit our knees in prayer. We become wise enough to ask Him to overrule any desire that would ultimately betray us. We no longer want anything that lacks His approval.

Why is the change of heart so important in the fulfillment of Psalm 37:4? Because hearts that do not delight in the Lord are destructive and deceitful. Jeremiah 17:9 says, "The heart is deceitful above all things and beyond cure." To be safe, God must transform the heart. Until we learn to delight ourselves in the Lord, we cannot trust the desires of our hearts. What our fleshly hearts want on their own can lead us to make the worst decisions of our lives. Can you remember a time when your heart led you down a destructive path? I certainly can. I want my heart's desire to reflect His desires.

Psalm 37:4 is a transforming Scripture. In our treasure hunt, we discover a new depth of relationship with God, an indescribable delight, and a safety valve for our hearts. Treasures worth hunting—no matter what our original motives may have been.

Praise

....

....

....

....

....

Repentance

....

....

....

....

....

Acknowledgment

....

....

....

....

....

Intercession

....

....

....

....

....

Supplication for Self

....

....

....

....

....

Equipping

....

....

....

....

....

Day Twenty

*"This, the first of his miraculous signs, Jesus performed at Cana in Galilee.
He thus revealed his glory, and his disciples put their faith in him" (John 2:11).*

Scripture Reading: John 2:1-11.

Christ performed many miracles during the time He tabernacled among us in human flesh. His first miracle was most assuredly significant. I believe the miracle He performed in Cana is still the most awesome wonder He performs for any willing seeker still chained to this earth: Christ fills empty vessels.

Nothing destroys life like emptiness. Hollow places deep inside of us never sit dormant. They are vacuums attempting to inhale anything within reach. Left unchecked, the clock will tick only so long before the life self-destructs. Christians are not exempt. We still battle overwhelming feelings of emptiness. We can possess eternal life yet never be "filled" with God's love.

Please heed this warning from one who knows: if Christ has not been invited to fill up all the hollow places in our lives, we may be saved—but we are not safe! Oswald Chambers said it beautifully: "No love of the natural heart is safe unless the human heart has been satisfied by God first."[8] How many of us have attempted to fill our hollow places with something other than God's love only to eventually find ourselves in trouble? My guess would be most of us.

How can we discover the safety of the fullness of God? Consider these two simple and practical actions.

- Fullness begins with honesty. Just as Mary stated the problem to Christ, tell Him what is missing in your life. Confess to Him your every vain attempt to fill it with things other than His love. Name every person and thing that has disappointed you and left you lacking. Recount to Him the cost of looking for love, acceptance, comfort, or healing in all the wrong places.
- Then, when you have been honest with your need, ask Him to fill you with His love and flood your life with His Spirit. NOT once and for all—but every day for the rest of your life.

When we allow Christ to fill our hollow places, inevitably others will draw closer to us. They will cease feeling as if we need more than they have to give. Only Christ can fill our empty pitchers. He is so anxious, so willing. He is the only One who will never be frightened by the depth of our need. Denying yourself does not mean denying your need. Denying yourself means denying you have the means to meet your need.

Praise

....

....

....

....

....

....

Repentance

....

....

....

....

....

Acknowledgment

....

....

....

....

....

Intercession

....

....

....

....

....

Supplication for Self

....

....

....

....

....

Equipping

....

....

....

....

....

J.D. MARSTON

Day Twenty-One

"Therefore everyone who hears these words of mine and puts them into practice is like a wise man who built his house on the rock" (Matt. 7:24).

Scripture Reading: Matthew 7:24-29

The first signs of dawn whispered me awake. I slipped out of bed, peeked through the heavy hotel-room curtains, and marveled at the sunrise I didn't want to miss. We were basking in some much-needed rest a thousand miles from home. I grabbed my journal, left the family sleeping, and hastened to spend time with the One who gave the seas their boundaries.

I slipped off my shoes to enjoy the cool, coarse sand beneath my feet, stood on the shore, and beheld the Artist at work. After God and I exchanged our glad good mornings, I glanced up and down the beach. No one in sight, yet I could see the remains of yesterday's sand castles. Parents and children alike worked for hours on structures doomed only to melt into the ocean. It was just a game. They knew it when they built them. But what our Scriptures describe today is not a game.

Notice the common denominators in the passage. Both men built a house. Both faced a storm. What is a house? Walls of protection, a refuge, a fortress, a place to rest and fellowship, often a place that defines our worth, our status. A place to call our own. Each of us builds a house for ourselves in one way or another.

Then came the storm. In every life what we've built is subject to raging winds and rising floods. They will come. Christ warns that the only indestructible house is the one built upon the rock of His teachings. The strength of our houses is not dependent upon our salvation. It's not dependent upon our faith. It's dependent upon our willingness to live according to God's Word. An unsettling thought indeed.

You see, we can be never-miss-a-church-service Christians but still never get "into" God's Word. Excuses like "I'm just not the studious type" don't cut it. We are a people desperate for God's Word. More than anything, God's people need to know His Word and be willing to give Him the freedom to adjust our lives to its precepts. Guarantees come from living our lives according to Scripture.

Yes, storms will come, but we have an absolute promise—our lives will not collapse. Every time we leave a Bible study or a sermon and methodically begin to discount the truth we've heard or apply it to others, a few shingles slide off our roofs, the sheet rock crumbles in a place or two, and our foundations crack just a little bit more.

But the best of news prevails. Every time we receive, believe, and heed His Word, He nails new shingles to our roofs, He reinforces our walls with fresh sheet rock, and His wet cement hardens beneath our feet. The storms come—but the house stands. As long as we have breath, it is never too late for a foolish man to become wise.

Better to have a hut on the Rock than a castle on the sand.

Praise

....

....

....

....

....

....

Repentance

....

....

....

....

....

....

Acknowledgment

....

....

....

....

....

....

Intercession

....

....

....

....

....

Supplication for Self

....

....

....

....

....

Equipping

....

....

....

....

....

Day Twenty-Two

"Therefore Jesus told them, 'The right time for me has not yet come; for you any time is right'" (John 7:6).

Scripture Reading: John 7:1-9

Sometimes we think of Christ's sufferings as limited to His final days on earth. We overlook the difficulties Jesus faced throughout His life. John 7 describes an ongoing conflict He faced. We wince when we read about the official who slapped Christ, but the sting couldn't compare to the emotional slap He received from His brothers.

Jesus "came unto his own, and his own received him not" (John 1:11, KJV). He suffered personal wounds long before a crown of thorns pierced His brow. Can you imagine the wonders Jesus' brothers missed because of their disbelief? When Christ confronted His brothers' ridicule, He taught them a vital lesson about timing. He can speak on the subject with authority. Time was the first element He created. Genesis 1:1 opens with the words, "In the beginning." Before Christ created light, He had to create time. Prior to creation, God the Father, God the Son, and God the Holy Spirit dwelt in timelessness. As the Creator of time, Christ can manipulate it as He chooses.

Enter timing—the manipulation of time. In Christ's rebuttal to His brothers, He drew a line in the sand separating them on the basis of their attitudes toward time. He said to them, "The right time for me has not yet come; for you any time is right."

Christ lived for one purpose: to do the will of the Father (see John 6:38). His brothers lived for themselves. One regarded time as a sacred tool to be used by the Father discriminately. The others perceived time as an invitation for opportunism at each man's discretion. The brothers' differences on the matter of timing measured a much deeper variance in the hearts of Mary's sons.

Perhaps today we can apply the same measuring stick to ourselves. Our attitude toward timing may shed light on the desires of our hearts. If our heart's desire is the will of God, we will wait for His timing even when the pause is long and uncomfortable. We gain nothing by running ahead of God. We remember times we've tried only to be displeased with the results. If we desire to do our own will, we will tend, like Christ's brothers, to think any time is right! Plunge ahead! Why wait on God?

John 7:5 tells us Christ's brothers "did not believe in him" at this time. Isn't it amazing how faith affects our attitudes about timing? Do we truly believe God knows what is best for us? Then we can also believe God knows when is best for us.

Are you waiting on God? Are you anxious because an answer is not coming? Remember no one uses timing better than the One who created time. Just because "the right time...has not yet come" doesn't mean you have to waste time. Use every second of the wait to allow the Father to increase your faith and deepen your trust. Stay so close that when He finally says "now," He'll only have to whisper.

Praise

....

....

....

....

....

....

Repentance

....

....

....

....

....

Acknowledgment

....

....

....

....

....

Intercession

....

....

....

....

....

Supplication for Self

....

....

....

....

....

Equipping

....

....

....

....

....

NICHOLAS PAVLOFF

Day Twenty-Three

*"At once I was in the Spirit, and there before me was a throne
in heaven with someone sitting on it" (Rev 4:2).*

Scripture Reading: Revelation 4

Limited by the stifling restraints of human language, the apostle John sought to describe the gloriously inconceivable through images we could see and understand. No matter how creative or artistic any one of us may be, our images of God's throne room will inevitably be awkward and crude. We have no vocabulary nor realm of experience from which to draw. Though the details and descriptions escape us, one characterization of John's glimpse of glory is crystal clear. In the center of it all is the throne of God. Look again. The apostle John delivered every description in its specific relationship to the throne of God. Clearly, everything else paled in comparison to the central focus of heaven. As soon as John arrived in Spirit, his first words were, "and there before me was a throne in heaven with someone sitting on it." Then he filled in the pencil portrait with the other inhabitants:

"A rainbow...encircled the throne.
Surrounding the throne were twenty-four other thrones....
From the throne came flashes of lightning....
Before the throne, seven lamps were blazing.
...before the throne there was what looked like a sea of glass....
In the center, around the throne, were four living creatures....
...the twenty-four elders fall down before him who sits on the throne....
They lay their crowns before the throne" (Rev. 4: 3-10).

You see, Beloved, from heaven's perspective everything is seen in relationship to the throne of God. Nothing stands alone because nothing can be understood apart from its relationship to the One on the throne.

God's Word offers great encouragement for us today. Each time Scripture gives a glimpse of the throne in heaven, it remains occupied. Take heart! You will never awaken to an upsetting morning headline like: "Vacancy Declared at God's Throne." You will never have to wonder if God is still occupying His throne. He never leaves His place. He never abdicates His authority nor resigns His role as Sovereign Ruler over heaven and earth. Not only is He always on the throne, things and events are viewed in the proper perspective only when seen in relationship to the One on His throne.

Your life, your family, your background, your health, your job, your service, your circumstances—how differently would you view these things if you could see them only in relationship to God on His throne? Any other outlook gives us blurry vision. Try a new way of looking at things—the only true way of looking at things.

Praise

....

....

....

....

....

Repentance

....

....

....

....

....

Acknowledgment

....

....

....

....

....

Intercession

....

....

....

....

....

....

Supplication for Self

....

....

....

....

....

....

Equipping

....

....

....

....

....

Day Twenty-Four

*"Then the Lord said to Moses, 'I will rain down bread from heaven for you.
The people are to go out each day and gather enough for that day. In this way I will
test them and see whether they will follow my instructions'" (Ex. 16:4).*

Scripture Reading: Exodus 16

The account of God supplying manna to the children of Israel is one of Scripture's most beautiful expressions of God's provision. He allowed His children to become hungry in a barren wilderness. They had neither means nor hope of acquiring food.

God certainly didn't intend to let His children starve, but He could have met their need in other ways. He could have caused the desert to produce vegetation—a small task for the Creator. He could have dulled their appetites and reduced their bodies' requirement for food—another small task for the One who formed the human body. Instead, He chose to rain down bread from heaven's kitchen six days a week for 40 years. They never had to ask. Surrounded by barrenness, they received plenty.

Tucked away in this marvelous chapter is a phrase we must not miss: "In this way I will test them." A constant dose of plenty can sometimes be a more difficult test than a constant dose of need. We have plenty—but we "need" more.

We in these United States live in a land of manna. Perhaps because our nation was founded on Christ, almost everyone can daily put something in their stomachs if only they will "go out and gather it up." But sometimes we forget that not everyone's daily supply is as simple to gather as our own may be. Inhabitants of other lands starve to death every day. We must not merely breathe a sigh of relief and be thankful we're not among them. Our plenty is a test.

What is the purpose of the test of plenty? According to Exodus 16:4, to "see whether they will follow my instructions." God is pinpointing an overwhelming tendency in human nature. We are far less likely to be obedient when we are not in need.

Necessity has a way of reordering our priorities, doesn't it? If we belong to Christ and find ourselves lacking, sooner or later we may begin evaluating whether or not we're living obedient lives God can bless. Coming face to face with need is a very effective prompter toward obedience. But what about a daily dose of plenty? I'm not referring to wealth—just the absence of worry as to whether or not our families will eat each week. Like the Israelites in the wilderness, our greatest dilemma is how we'll cook and serve our manna today—not whether we'll have the manna.

Herein lies the test. Must we be in immediate need to live obedient lives?

God is so faithful. So daily. Oh, how He delights in obedience prompted from something deeply internal—a heart of love and devotion. Ask Him today to help you become a child of God whose levels of obedience are less regulated by circumstances and more governed by love.

Praise

....

....

....

....

....

....

Repentance

....

....

....

....

....

Acknowledgment

....

....

....

....

....

Intercession

....

....

....

....

....

Supplication for Self

....

....

....

....

....

Equipping

....

....

....

....

....

NICHOLAS PAVLOFF

Day Twenty-Five

"Put away perversity from your mouth;
keep corrupt talk far from your lips" (Prov. 4:24).

Scripture Reading: Proverbs 4:24-27; Isaiah 6:5

Like the prophet Isaiah, we live "among a people of unclean lips" (Isa. 6:5). Perverse language and corrupt talk so inundates our culture that we risk growing desensitized. How many times have we turned on the television and been shocked that a certain word was allowed to travel the public airways?

We grow accustomed to hearing one word just in time to hear another. In the name of entertainment, we have slowly and sometimes unknowingly lowered our standards. If we do not take great care to resist, we will likewise become men and women of "unclean lips."

What we hear has tremendous impact on how we talk. My thick Tex-Arkansan accent is a good example. I can't cross the Texas border without being asked, "Where in the world are you from?" I had no intention of developing another accent when I moved to Texas, but the more I heard the twang, the more I spoke the language.

Our physical accents are affected by the regions in which we live. Our spiritual accents are also affected by the areas we choose to occupy. God desires and expects both our speech and our figures of speech to glorify Him. As perverse language and corrupt talk increases around us, we must work hard to stay a people of clean lips. The apostle Paul reminds us that "our citizenship is in heaven" (Phil. 3:20). God wants our speech to give away where we're from.

We reveal our true home not by religious jargon people can't understand, but by purity of speech—and by pure default! Sometimes simply refusing to talk the way the world talks is a powerful witnessing tool.

Let's allow God to give us a swig of mouthwash when necessary—like when we're angry, or when we're trying to make a powerful point, or even when we're simply trying to be funny. In Christ, we can find ways to deal with anger, make a point, and enjoy humor without compromising our speech. God can help us to break old habits and form new ones. One way we can do that is to spend time with people who talk with "accents" we admire.

Who are two people whose speech you admire?

What about their manner of speaking impresses you?

What one specific thing could you do to become more like them in your speech?

As each of us raises our own personal standard of expression, it won't be long until somebody asks us, "Where in the world are you from?"

Praise

....

....

....

....

....

....

Repentance

....

....

....

....

....

....

Acknowledgment

....

....

....

....

....

....

Intercession

···

···

···

···

···

···

Supplication for Self

···

···

···

···

···

Equipping

···

···

···

···

···

Day Twenty-Six

Jesus answered, "It is written: 'Man does not live on bread alone,
but on every word that comes from the mouth of God'" (Matt. 4:4).

Scripture Reading: Matthew 4:1-11

Every believer in Christ will experience occasional intense confrontations with the enemy. At such times Satan's persistence can seem overwhelming. Scripture records Jesus' 40-day encounter with the tempter so we can learn a lesson from His success. Christ won His battle with His highly skilled use of God's Word. Ephesians 6:17 calls the Word the "sword of the Spirit." Scripture is the only offensive weapon we have against the evil one. The other pieces of armor described in Ephesians 6 are defensive in nature. The enemy can be relentless in his attack. If we're going to be victorious during times of intense battle, we need to take some lessons from Christ, the ultimate Swordsman. Here are a few tips based on His example.

Familiarize yourself with Scripture. We don't come equipped with a knowledge of Scripture. We must study it. Such study doesn't mean just learning biblical history. Bible study involves a relationship with a person. "The Word became flesh and made his dwelling among us" (John 1:14). Christ didn't just learn the Word; He is the Word!

Memorize Scriptures. Christ didn't pull out His pocket Torah in the desert and start flipping pages. We don't always have our Bibles in easy reach. We need a quick-draw supply of Scriptures hidden in our heart for times we face temptation. Psalm 119:11 says, "I have hidden your word in my heart that I might not sin against you."

Learn how to apply Scripture. Christ answered His adversary with specific Scriptures applying to each temptation. Learn to respond to the enemy with Scriptures aimed specifically at your temptation or battle. I remember a time when I stood boldly on the Word of God. The problem was I rarely climbed off and opened it. I claimed to believe something I knew little about. We can't stand on a closed Bible. We must open it, learn it, and apply it. A Bible concordance is a great resource tool for helping you locate Scriptures pertaining to a particular need.

Be persistent. If the enemy isn't backing off, you have no choice but to keep fighting. He didn't tuck his tail and run the first time Christ drew the Sword of the Spirit. We can be pretty certain he's not going to back off easily from us. A simple rebuke doesn't always work when we're walking through a season of spiritual warfare.

First Corinthians 10:11 says of the Israelites' experiences, "These things happened to them as examples and were written down as warnings for us."

In context, the apostle Paul was referring specifically to lessons from poor examples. God provided us with four Gospels recording Jesus' earthly life so we could also learn from a perfect example.

Christ can handle a sword. Let's make sure we've signed up for lessons.

Praise

....
....
....
....
....
....

Repentance

....
....
....
....
....
....

Acknowledgment

....
....
....
....
....

Intercession

....

....

....

....

....

Supplication for Self

....

....

....

....

....

Equipping

....

....

....

....

....

J.D. MARSTON

Day Twenty-Seven

"Your word, O Lord, is eternal; it stands firm in the heavens" (Ps. 119:89).

Scripture Reading: Psalm 119:89-96

We live in the age of information. The resources available at our fingertips are staggering. "Professional" advice pours from our radios and televisions. The Internet offers a wealth of data. We can access health tips, financial tips, relationship tips, fashion tips—tips on parenting to plumbing. If you have the time, they have the tips. There's only one hitch—by the time you opt to change, they're apt to change.

Yesterday's software demands today's upgrade. When the time comes to purchase a new printer cartridge, one look from the indignant salesperson tells you they don't make your model anymore. Yesterday's health tips are today's horrors.

We are bombarded by information fluctuation. Are we truly making advances? How should we rear our families? Our parents' and grandparents' sound parenting ideas are assaulted by today's experts. We scramble to readjust our methods only to learn that the rules have changed. Before we know it, we'll be the bad guys, and look who is giving us advice! Single talk-show hosts offer marriage counseling, and people obviously under the influence of hallucinogens provide fashion advice. Scary, isn't it?

As the information whirlwind swirls around us, we have an anchor in the Word of God. All the peace seekers in the world can't write a better thesis on community living than the Ten Commandments. All the psychiatrists in the yellow pages can't write a better emotional health plan than biblical forgiveness and divine healing. All the financial advisers on Wall Street can't suggest wiser money management than the Book of Proverbs. Marital advice? Sexual fulfillment? Guidelines on business partnerships? How to be single and happy? It's all there. Better yet, it never needs an upgrade.

God's Word stands the test of time and was written purposely to pertain to every generation. Why? Because His counsel applies regardless of changes in our lives.

My grandmother grew up in the late 1800s. She was reared on the principles in God's Word. She survived the loss of both parents, the poverty of the Great Depression, and the death of her husband and three young children by clinging to what she called her "testament." She witnessed the change of a century, yet when she died in 1973 she never could have imagined the world of the new millennium.

Though a society foreign to hers complicates our lives, the Word of God remains adequate for her grandchildren and their children. We have no idea what awaits future generations. Nuclear disaster? Cure for cancer? Economic collapse? Colonization of the moon? We do not know. Times will change—but God's Word remains solid. Look to the legacy of timeless advice, to those tips that will last when today's technology is a laugh from the past—"Heaven and earth will pass away, but my words will never pass away" (Matt. 24:35).

Praise

....

....

....

....

....

....

Repentance

....

....

....

....

....

Acknowledgment

....

....

....

....

Intercession

....

....

....

....

....

....

Supplication for Self

....

....

....

....

....

Equipping

....

....

....

....

....

Day Twenty-Eight

"Jesus knew that the Father had put all things under his power,
and that he had come from God and was returning to God;
so he...began to wash his disciples' feet" (John 13:3-5).

Scripture Reading: John 13:1-17

Imagine Christ appearing before you this very moment, kneeling on the floor, and washing your feet. Not a very comfortable thought, is it? Can you relate to Peter's impulsive statement, "You shall never wash my feet" (John 13:8)? I once struggled over what to do with the gift of a pedicure! Feet don't belong in anyone else's hands! If you ask me that's why they are fastened to the ankle instead of the wrist.

Christ's actions stunned the disciples. The lowliest servant in the house washed feet. Had Christ asked for one of them to wash His feet, I doubt He would have had any takers. In Luke's version of the same meal, "a dispute arose among them as to which of them was considered to be greatest" (Luke 22:24). We can be fairly certain that this "dispute" led to a foot-washing lesson on servanthood.

Through this unforgettable act, Christ shed light on the disciples' differences. They wanted position; He wanted possession. They wanted importance; He wanted witnesses. They did agree on one goal, however; they wanted greatness and He wanted to grant it—His way. In Mark 10:43-44 Christ said, "whoever wants to become great among you must be your servant, and whoever wants to be first must be slave of all."

Like us, the disciples often liked Christ's goals but disliked His methods. Christ's standard for true servanthood? In Mark 10:45 He said, "the Son of Man did not come to be served, but to serve." We, like the disciples, want to be leaders. Perhaps we don't particularly want the responsibility of leadership, but we wouldn't mind the status. We like the idea of being well-respected and highly esteemed. The New Testament says very little about leadership but contains volumes about servanthood. By both word and deed Christ proclaims: my leaders are my servants.

Why are we so reluctant to humble ourselves with foot-washing attitudes of service? A key reason is because we suffer from an identity crisis. We still define ourselves by others' perceptions and reactions. Christ could wash grimy feet because He knew who He was. He could get on His knees and serve a bunch of self-serving saps because His identity came from the Father. He knew who He was to God.

The more we know God through prayer and His Word, the more aware of and comfortable with our true identity we'll become. It won't matter if others highly esteem us. We'll gladly humble ourselves before them because we are highly esteemed by One much greater.

As strange as it seems, Christ does have our future greatness in mind. He grants it to those who have lived their lives humbly—with a lap full of feet.

Praise

....

....

....

....

....

....

Repentance

....

....

....

....

....

Acknowledgment

....

....

....

....

....

Intercession

....
....
....
....
....
....

Supplication for Self

....
....
....
....
....
....

Equipping

....
....
....
....
....

NICHOLAS PAVLOFF

Day Twenty-Nine

"My son, do not make light of the Lord's discipline, and do not lose heart when he rebukes you, because the Lord disciplines those he loves" (Heb. 12:5-6).

Scripture Reading: Hebrews 12:4-13

The Lord is a disciplinarian. Never doubt it. He is far too faithful to let us get away with some of the things we think, say, and do. He has obligated Himself to grow us, be glorified in us, and give us away to His Son as a fitting bride "made... ready" (Rev. 19:7). Completing the good work He began in us demands discipline.

What definition of discipline does the writer intend? Take another look at verse 11. We can describe the Lord's discipline as His means of teaching profitable lessons in painful ways. Granted, some are more painful than others. The writer of Hebrews offers us wonderful encouragements in the midst of discipline. Let's consider a few.

God only disciplines those He loves. Today's text gives us reason to be concerned if we've never experienced the Lord's discipline. If you have, Beloved, count yourself among His children. Unbelievers sometimes experience God's wrath but, according to Hebrews 12, only His children undergo His discipline. How do we know the difference? Wrath is condemning in nature. Discipline is correcting in nature.

God always disciplines with expertise. He is the expert parent and disciplinarian. "Our fathers disciplined us...as they thought best" (v. 10). God disciplines us because He knows best. Unlike us, God won't have parenting regrets. He doesn't get wiser with age. He won't someday be a grandparent who says, "I wish I knew then what I know now." He is omniscient. He sees every detail, He knows every motive, He reads every thought, and He discerns every heart. He applies His loving discipline perfectly.

God never disciplines without profit in mind. Hebrews 12:11,13 lists at least three benefits discipline brings the teachable child: righteousness, peace, and healing. The straightforward approach of Proverbs 12:1 makes me laugh, "He who hates correction is stupid." No wonder. Look at those gains!

In my late 30s, with fear and trepidation, I began to ask God to be strict with me. I saw that His ways produce constant wins and my ways produce only losses. I deeply desired to live the holy life and to glorify Him. This remains my ongoing pursuit and my daily struggle. As the apostle Paul said: "I do not consider myself yet to have taken hold of it. But...I press on" (Phil. 3:13-14).

God is presently doing what I asked Him to do. He is very strict with me, and I never attempt to cross a line that I don't find Him standing on it. In order to cross it, I have to absolutely defy His authority. I've never been so disciplined—and I've never been so free. I am still capable of defying Him horribly but, if I dare, I pray His loving discipline will jerk me home.

Oh, beloved child of God, Father knows best.

Praise

....

....

....

....

....

Repentance

....

....

....

....

....

Acknowledgment

....

....

....

....

....

Intercession

Supplication for Self

Equipping

Day Thirty

"As he approached Jerusalem and saw the city, he wept over it and said, 'If you, even you, had only known on this day what would bring you peace'" (Luke 19:41-42).

Scripture Reading: Luke 19:28-44

We often make the mistake of imagining Christ as virtually emotionless—not really happy, not really sad. Just steady. In stark contrast, the Word of God describes a refreshingly emotional man—yet uniquely perfect.

English Scripture translations are often less descriptive than the Hebrew and Greek texts. As we dig into the original descriptions of Christ's emotions, we discover that He sometimes danced and leaped with great joy. We also learn that He grieved—and not simply with tears streaming down His cheeks. He expressed real-live, fit-throwing grief. In fact, the original word for Jesus' weeping in verse 41 is *klaio*, "implying not only the shedding of tears, but also every external expression of grief."[9]

Keep in mind the Hebrew people were quite demonstrative. No one had to teach them to express their feelings! You may be wondering what would upset Christ enough to make Him act out "every external expression of grief." Was it Lazarus' death? No. Was it His agony in the garden of Gethsemane? No. Was it the abandonment by His disciples? Not that either. You've just read the account in Luke 19:41-42. Let's insert the definition: "As he approached Jerusalem and saw the city, he *[expressed every external expression of grief]* over it." Why? Because Jerusalem had refused the Prince of peace. The city of Zion is still in turmoil for the same reason. Sadly, so are many Christians. Christ cannot bear to see us in constant turbulence.

If you knew you were going to die tonight, what treasure would you leave your loved ones? Something valuable to you, I'm sure. Just before His crucifixion, Christ said: "Peace I leave with you; my peace I give you. I do not give to you as the world gives. Do not let your hearts be troubled and do not be afraid" (John 14:27). In this verse Jesus left something immensely valuable—peace.

Can you think of a time when Christ's peace empowered you to deal with a situation that in normal circumstances would have left you out of control? If so, praise Him for it. Can you think of a time when you needed Christ's peace but you felt isolated? If so, what could you learn from the experience?

For reasons pertaining to eternal glory, Christ may not instantly remove your pain, your thorn, or your sickness, but, Beloved, regardless of the trial, you can receive His peace. It is your legacy. Your inheritance. Your right. You need not remain in turmoil. Nothing breaks His heart more than our refusal to be at peace in Him.

Christ offers you peace. Today and everyday. Claim it now.

Praise

....

....

....

....

....

Repentance

....

....

....

....

....

Acknowledgment

....

....

....

....

....

Intercession

....

....

....

....

....

....

Supplication for Self

....

....

....

....

....

....

Equipping

....

....

....

....

....

NICHOLAS PAVLOFF

Day Thirty-One

"Then God said, 'Take your son, your only son, Isaac, whom you love, and go to the region of Moriah. Sacrifice him there as a burnt offering on one of the mountains I will tell you about'" (Gen. 22:2).

Scripture Reading: Genesis 22:1-19

Isn't today's Scripture disturbing? We know that "from everyone who has been given much, much will be demanded" (Luke 12:48), but we'll gladly step aside and allow another to be called faithful if this is the kind of sacrifice it takes. However, we can't step aside quite as far as we'd like. We have more in common with Abram, "the father of a multitude of nations" (Gen. 17:5, NASB), than we might think. Consider a few comparisons.

First of all, our most profound tests involve those dearest to us. You know it's true; you've been there. Each of us can vividly remember a time when God called upon us to surrender our hold and our ownership over someone we love—perhaps even someone we nearly worship.

Second, we also experience times when we believe we've received two seemingly diametrically opposite messages from God. Abram understood God to say he would have more offspring than the number of stars in the sky. Then he received the command to sacrifice his only legitimate heir on the altar. As we continually trust the One who called us, we will eventually recognize that God truly is Reconciler of the utterly irreconcilable.

You see, God didn't mislead Abram. He told him to sacrifice his son on the altar and, most assuredly, Abram did. He did not slay his son. Instead, he was able to offer God a living sacrifice. Mind you, living sacrifices are not always easy to offer either. Sometimes releasing our grip on the person who remains with us can be a more painful test than releasing our grip on the person taken from our reach. We're presented with an ongoing test during which we must continually offer our precious ones to the One who loves them most.

I see a final comparison. God used Abraham and Isaac to teach others about Himself. The substitutionary offering of the ram caught by its horns in the thicket became one of the Bible's key images to convey the gospel message. The shadow of the cross fell on Mount Moriah that day. We all have been tied to the altar of death and then presented a chance to be loosed for eternal life by the perfect Lamb, One whose head was torn by thorns and was willing to take our place.

Our present challenges may not be as dramatic as Abram's, but we, too, can allow our lives to become visual aids through which God teaches others about Himself—and His faithful ways. I ask you now to read on the following page the words God gave me during a time when He led me to my own Mount Moriah. Only you know how this message applies to you. Please allow God to speak to your heart.

Trust Me with Your Isaac

For every Abraham who dares
to kiss the foreign field
where glory for a moment grasped
Is for a lifetime tilled...

The voice of God
speaks not but once
but 'til the traveler hears
"Abraham! Abraham! Bring your
Isaac here!"

"Bring not the blemished sacrifice.
What lovest thou the most?
Look not into the distance,
you'll find your Isaac close."

"I hear the tearing of your heart
torn between two loves,
the one your vision can behold
the Other hid above."

"Do you trust me, Abraham
with your gravest fear?
Will you pry your fingers loose
and bring your Isaac here?"

"Have I not made you promises?
Hold them tight instead!
I am the Lover of your soul—
the Lifter of your head."

"Believe me, O my Abraham
when blinded by the cost.
Arrange the wooded altar
and count your gains but loss."

"Let tears wash clean your blinded eyes
until unveiled you see—
the ram caught in the thicket there
to set your Isaac free."

"Perhaps I'll send him down the mount
to walk right by your side.
No longer in your iron grasp
but safer still in mine."

"Or I may wrap him in the wind
and sweep him from your sight
to better things beyond your reach—
believe with all your might!"

"Look up, beloved Abraham.
Can you count the stars?
Multitudes will stand to reap
from one dear friend of God."

"Pass the test, my faithful one;
bow to me as Lord.
Trust me with your Isaac—
see,
I am your great Reward."

Praise

....

....

....

....

....

Repentance

....

....

....

....

....

Acknowledgment

....

....

....

....

....

Intercession

Supplication for Self

Equipping

Day Thirty-Two

"Who is this that darkens my counsel with words without knowledge?" (Job 38:2).

Scripture Reading: Job 38:1-41; 40:1-5

By any chance have you recently forgotten that God is God? Like Job and his counselors, have you ever received a fresh reality check from God? I have! When God sees me becoming a little too presumptuous, He carefully reestablishes our roles.

My children would probably be glad to know I've had a taste of my own medicine. You see, on a far smaller scale, I've been on the other side of this conflict for control. I have a very strong-willed child who, in her mother's biased opinion, is one of the most wonderful creatures God ever placed upon this earth. As dearly as I love her, every couple of months, almost like clockwork, we go around the bend. She was born a leader and began practicing her skills on our family immediately. We frequently have to reestablish who is boss.

Usually my precious daughter remains within acceptable boundaries. Her slightly presumptuous personality is rather endearing and often hilarious—but gradually she begins the next coup attempt. It starts with a little attitude. Left alone, the attitude morphs into full-blown audacity that leads to the inevitable blowup—usually mine.

The explosion always comes with the same words: "Now hear this: I am your mother. I AM YOUR BOSS. GOT THAT?" She bursts into tears, probably writes me a mean letter I never see, tells her Daddy on me (who later laughs at us), sleeps on it, and awakens the next morning as gentle as a lamb. Okay—maybe a goat—but the cutest goat you've ever seen. And we start all over.

I believe God sometimes experiences a similar tug-of-war with us. He loves us with all His heart and finds us extremely endearing. Yes, even hilarious at times. Then we begin our attempted coups—we want to take over. How does it start? Like it starts with my daughter. We start with a little attitude. Then the attitude finds its way out of our mouths. That's when God says something like, "Who is this that darkens my counsel with words without knowledge?" I would say: "You don't know what you're talking about." If unchecked, the attitude turns into full-blown audacity, at which point we can be pretty certain God will deal with us—not like a wicked judge but like a loving parent, intent on rearing a respectful child.

Look back over the questions God asked His temporarily presumptuous son, Job, in chapter 38. Which was your personal favorite? Memorize it as I memorize mine—and every time the Spirit of God convicts us of audacity, let's imagine hearing the same question straight from His lips. Sometimes when God asserts His "God-ness" to pull us back into proper bounds, we get our feelings hurt and throw a fit. Then, if He really owns our hearts, we return to Him with a fresh meekness, as gentle as a lamb—or maybe a goat—but a cute goat.

Praise

....

....

....

....

....

....

Repentance

....

....

....

....

....

....

Acknowledgment

....

....

....

....

....

Intercession

....

....

....

....

....

Supplication for Self

....

....

....

....

....

Equipping

....

....

....

....

NICHOLAS PAVLOFF

Day Thirty-Three

"Then Moses said to him, 'If your Presence does not go with us,
do not send us up from here'" (Ex. 33:15).

Scripture Reading: Exodus 33:1-17

Moses had a remarkable relationship with God. The Scriptures tell us "the Lord would speak to Moses face to face" (v. 11). Moses did not see God's face (see Ex. 33:23), rather he experienced an indescribable level of intimacy that comes from two having their full attentions and expressions turned toward each other. "The Lord would speak to Moses...as a man speaks with his friend" (v. 11).

Mind you, the Scripture doesn't say Moses spoke to God as one speaks to a friend. The amazing statement is that God spoke to Moses as a man speaks to his friend. The passage describes God talking friend-talk. I can hardly fathom it. So deeply involved were God and Moses that the weary servant could not bear the thought of proceeding a single step without God's presence.

God promised Moses He would send a mighty angel before them and guide them to their God-given destiny. He assured Moses of success—but Moses didn't want good results. He wanted God. The old man's example raises quite a standard for us today. Would we be content for God to simply assure us of personal success and victory in reaching our divine destinies? What if He also promised the security of a mighty angel constantly paving the way and fighting our battles for us? And what if there was just one catch—we would not experience the closeness of God's presence? How would you feel if God promised you success and victory but without His presence?

Would we know the difference? Would we go on reluctantly? Or would we trade in every victory, every dream come true—our chosen destiny—just to enjoy His presence? Difficult questions. But I think if we knew God—really knew Him so well He felt He could talk to us like a friend and share HIS heart with us as we share ours with Him—we would trade in everything just to enjoy His presence.

Once we grow accustomed to God's presence in our lives and He becomes our most intimate companion, we are inconsolable outside His presence. By presence I'm not referring to salvation; I'm referring to a sense of His presence through a face-to-face, intimate relationship. We will not desire anything to quench the awareness of His nearness. And when we do smother that awareness with our own selfishness, we will run with repentance. We will not want to make a move without receiving an answer to this question: "Is Your presence going with me, God? If not, keep me in the wilderness, seal away the milk and honey, keep the Jordan from my sight. For if Your presence does not go with me, do not send me from here."

The land of promise is the land of His presence. Without Him, what, indeed, sets anything apart?

Praise

....

....

....

....

....

....

Repentance

....

....

....

....

....

Acknowledgment

....

....

....

....

....

Intercession

....

....

....

....

....

Supplication for Self

....

....

....

....

....

Equipping

....

....

....

....

....

Day Thirty-Four

*"I tell you, though he will not get up and give him the bread
because he is his friend, yet because of the man's boldness he will get up
and give him as much as he needs" (Luke 11:8).*

Scripture Reading: Luke 11:1-10

The parable of the gutsy friend is one of the most unique parallels Jesus ever drew. Please don't miss the context of Christ's lesson on boldness. The disciples begged, "Lord, teach us to pray" (Luke 11:1). Believers have great familiarity with the prayer that followed, but in the very next breath Christ taught the parable of the relentless friend. In other words: "And when you pray, pray boldly! Pray persistently!"

You may be as uncomfortable as I once was at this sort of boldness in prayer. The seeker seemed a nuisance. I thought, *I don't want God to feel He must throw something out the door to me because I won't stop annoying Him.* Don't miss the relationship between the seeker and the giver in this parable. They were friends—not just neighbors. The relationship is vital to the story. The parable never suggests a bold stranger would have received a similar response.

In Greek, *friends* "share common interests." So the seeker was not asking something contrary to the giver's interests. The giver might have preferred to lend his friend the loaves the next morning, but he certainly was unopposed to granting his request. The parable does not teach that God will give us anything we ask if we are bold enough. "Friends" do not ask of others what they would be opposed to giving. Friends know one another well enough to discern whether requests are appropriate. In this wonderful parable Christ invited us to pray with boldness and persistence as a "friend" of God—one who shares His common interests.

When I think of this parable, a friend comes to mind. Joy and her husband had a son who went through a head-strong season during high school. One evening they forbade him to go out with his rebellious friends—he turned on his heels and walked out the door anyway. His parents were heartbroken. The next day the son angrily demanded of his mother, "Have you been praying for me again in my room?"

She finally replied: "Son, I always pray for you. Why do you ask?"

His answer has stuck with me: "Because there were elbow prints on my bedspread!"

Elbow prints conveyed a mother's prayers as she knelt by his bed and begged for his release. Soon the son could no longer bear the strain. He returned to his loving parents and grew to be a godly husband and father. His sons are still young, but if either rebels, their actions may be no match for a father's prayers at their bedside.

Do you have a concern that is also God's interest? Are you His "friend" in this matter, not asking for selfish reasons? Then keep asking. Go boldly before the throne.

Leave a few elbow prints on the bedspread. He hears you.

Praise

....

....

....

....

....

....

Repentance

....

....

....

....

....

Acknowledgment

....

....

....

....

....

Intercession

....

....

....

....

....

....

Supplication for Self

....

....

....

....

....

....

Equipping

....

....

....

....

....

NICHOLAS PAVLOFF

Day Thirty-Five

"And without faith it is impossible to please God" (Heb. 11:6).

Scripture Reading: Hebrews 11:1-6

Have you ever wondered why you seem to get one faith walk—times when you must walk by faith rather than by sight—behind you just in time to begin another? Because "without faith it is impossible to please God!"

Revelation 4:11 proclaims our Creator's purpose, "Thou hast created all things, and for thy pleasure they are and were created" (KJV). We were created for our Creator's pleasure and the building of our faith gives Him pleasure.

If you are really candid, you may be thinking: *Why should the point of life be God's pleasure? What kind of egotistical deity is He?* God's motive is not selfish. Take another look at Hebrews 11:6. He wants to reward those who exercise faith—those who "earnestly seek Him" even when they cannot "see" Him. God's pleasure is to bless and reward His children and to lift them to spiritual heights they've never imagined. He wants to prepare us for the place in which He is accumulating treasures in our behalf as we walk victoriously in faith.

Hebrews 11:1 tells us, "Now faith is being sure of what we hope for and certain of what we do not see." Our greatest reality—in other words that which is most "real"—is that which cannot be seen with human eyes. Think about it. How do your circumstances or your present challenges "look" to you right now? Based only on the evidences surrounding your deepest concern, how might you assume things are going to work out?

Hebrews 11 reminds us that the most influential factors determining outcome in the life of believers are those we cannot see. Your greatest reality in your greatest difficulty is an invisible, all-powerful God. Learn to look at your faith walks from His point of view: He is directing or allowing circumstances for the sheer purpose of rewarding you. The test is whether or not you'll seek His invisible face. The reward is beyond your comprehension. Why so many faith walks? Because He has so much to give! And, frankly, so little time. Your walk in the fleeting "here and now" has colossal influence over His reward in your "there and forever."

To give to you is God's greatest pleasure, but He does "not give to you as the world gives" (John 14:27). Every reward this world can offer is here on earth "where moth and rust destroy, and where thieves break in and steal" (Matt. 6:20). God, however, is interested in quality. Every reward He has for you carries an eternal lifetime guarantee. One day the visible will be invisible and the unseen seen—instantly.

Look around you for a moment. Everything you see will disintegrate. "Behold, I am coming soon! My reward is with me" (Rev. 22:12). That's reality. This life is only a vapor.

Praise

....

....

....

....

....

....

Repentance

....

....

....

....

....

Acknowledgment

....

....

....

....

....

Intercession

....

....

....

....

....

Supplication for Self

....

....

....

....

....

Equipping

....

....

....

....

....

Day Thirty-Six

"He persevered because he saw him who is invisible" (Heb. 11:27).

Scripture Reading: Hebrews 11:24-27

Today we will continue yesterday's theme of faith. How we define and exercise faith makes all the difference in our lives. Believers in Christ must place their faith in one of two factors: either what God does or who God is.

If we place our faith in what God is doing, we should brace ourselves for a life-long roller-coaster ride. Our faith will be high and mighty one day and free-falling the next because it is based on the apparent activity of God in our circumstances. Remember, God warns us in Isaiah 55:9, "As the heavens are higher than the earth, so are my ways higher than your ways." If we define *faith* based on our ability to discern what God is doing, we are bound for a ride on the *Sky Screamer.*

In many of life's circumstances, we can't begin to understand what God is doing. When He chooses to take a beloved servant home to heaven rather than healing him on earth, our faith disintegrates because it's based on what God appears to be doing.

Remember that most of what God does is invisible—totally outside our realm of observation or understanding. We cannot base our faith on what He appears to be doing or how dramatically He answers our prayers—because faith founded on God's apparent actions is not faith at all. Attempting to exercise our faith according to what we can see cancels out that very faith.

Remember Hebrews 11:1, "Now faith is being...certain of what we do not see." Our faith must rest on God's identity, not His activity.

Hebrews 11:6 highlights a vital element in genuine faith—believing God exists and earnestly seeking HIM. In our most difficult losses, victory does not result from seeking God's answers nor His activity. Many answers will never come; much of His activity will never be seen. Victorious faith walks evolve from seeking Him.

In Hebrews 11:27 we read that Moses "persevered because he saw him who is invisible"—not because he saw the burning bush. He gazed straight into the face of the invisible God. He built his faith on Who God is, not what God had done.

God performed unparalleled miracles in Moses' life, yet still His servant was more preoccupied with knowing God than seeing His activity. You see, seeking a God we cannot "see" is real, live faith. It's also our ticket off the roller coaster.

God's activity may appear to change, but Who He is will never change. Jesus is "the same yesterday and today and forever" (Heb. 13:8). When you don't know what God is doing, you can find stability in Who He is. The more you know about Him, the more you'll be able to hang on when life feels as if it's in the derailment mode.

Climb off the roller coaster. Life offers so many opportunities to enjoy what God is doing—but we must rely on Who God is.

Praise

....

....

....

....

....

Repentance

....

....

....

....

....

Acknowledgment

....

....

....

....

....

Intercession

....

....

....

....

....

Supplication for Self

....

....

....

....

....

Equipping

....

....

....

....

....

NICHOLAS PAVLOFF

Day Thirty-Seven

"For when one says, 'I follow Paul,' and another, 'I follow Apollos,'
are you not mere men?" (1 Cor. 3:4).

Scripture Reading: 1 Corinthians 1:10-17; 3:1-9

Regarding His church, nothing means more to Christ than unity; obviously Satan's priority work is division. The enemy already knows the gates of hell cannot prevail against the church (see Matt. 16:18), so instead he attacks from the inside.

Satan knows that Jesus said, "every...household divided against itself will not stand" (Matt. 12:25). Though Satan cannot overcome the church as a whole, he wreaks havoc and excludes many by cultivating division from the inside out.

In Joshua 3, God told Joshua and the children of Israel how to enter the promised land. The Israelites had grown comfortable in their "camps," but when the waters parted they had to cross as one. As God promised, the waters heaped and "all Israel passed by until the whole nation had completed the crossing on dry ground" (Josh. 3:17).

As God yearned to take the Israelites to the place He promised, Christ yearns to take His church to her place of destiny. One day "she" will rule with Him on earth and take her privileged position as the bride of Christ. Until that time, He wants to mature His church and work mightily through her in this age.

If I may say so gently, it's time for the church to grow up. We desperately need to break up a few camps in Christ's church and let Him move us on to maturity. We have denominational camps, fundamentalist camps, conservative camps, moderate camps, liberal camps. We have camps within a camp. Our church staffs, meant to be examples of unity, are often replete with camps. Church members stand behind this minister against that minister—the division goes on and on and on.

The church in Corinth was acting like a pimple-faced school girl who couldn't decide which "guy" she liked best. The Corinthian believers were at odds over whether to follow Paul, Apollos, or Peter. Never one to mince words, in effect Paul said: "The question is whether or not you follow Christ! No one else matters!" In other words, break up the camps and move on to maturity!

By no means did Paul call for a church with no human leadership. He proposed a church with no human lordship. Let's allow God to turn our hearts inside out. Do we have human leaders we respect—or human "lords" we worship? Are we in Christ's camp and His alone? Or, have we lined up to swear by a flesh-and-blood leader? Oh, Believer, be very careful to whom you swear your allegiance. Peter, Paul, and Apollos were all trustworthy leaders; yet God's Word still warned the early church to refrain from dividing in camps behind them.

Christ is the Head of the church, and we are unified only as we all bend our knees to Him. May we be "brought to complete unity" (John 17:23).

Praise

....
....
....
....
....
....

Repentance

....
....
....
....
....
....

Acknowledgment

....
....
....
....
....

Intercession

....

....

....

....

....

Supplication for Self

....

....

....

....

....

Equipping

....

....

....

....

....

Day Thirty-Eight

"Therefore he is able to save completely those who come to God through him, because he always lives to intercede for them" (Heb. 7:25).

Scripture Reading: Hebrews 7:23-28

Have you wondered just what Christ is doing while He awaits the Father's signal to return for His bride? He's not just twiddling holy thumbs nor frozen in indignation over the follies of men. Christ is very much at work in the here and now.

Hebrews 7:25 states one of Christ's priority works on our behalf—He "lives to intercede for" us. The word translated *save* refers to "any kind of deliverance." Considering the context and the parallel to the high priests over the nation of Israel, this verse may refer most readily to believers in Christ. The Son of God occupies the seat at the right hand of God where He is the designated High Priest, the divine Intercessor for His people. Christ "lives" to pray for us.

The original meaning of the word *intercedes* is very significant. The verb *eutugchano* "means to interpolate with familiarity and freedom of access, to interrupt another in speaking, to come to God with boldness."[10] Consider briefly the wonderful elements of Christ's intercession. First, He prays for us with familiarity. He is completely familiar with the Father and with us. He prays for us with complete knowledge and understanding of God's perfect will, His ultimate plan, our deepest desires, and our greatest needs. He qualifies, therefore, as the perfect "go-between."

Second, Christ has total freedom of access. So do we because Christ paved the way for us, but His physical position at His Father's right hand and His familial position as the Father's beloved Son grants Him a freedom of access unlike any other! Beloved, revel in knowing Christ uses His "freedom of access" on your behalf.

The third element in the definition is most intriguing. How does intercession involve "interrupting another in speaking"? I believe one of Christ's greatest acts of intercession involves interrupting the feeble prayers of His people with familiarity, freedom, and confidence! I believe He is looking for people on their knees in prayer, so He can interrupt sincere but impotent petitions with the power of the heavenlies!

Our great High Priest lives to empower our prayer lives. However, if we're going to release Christ to do His fullest work as High Priest, we must first offer earnest prayer He can interrupt. How can He interrupt someone who is not praying?

Finally, the verse explains that Christ "comes to God with boldness." Though He invites us to approach the throne boldly, we often have difficulty discerning where boldness ends and bossiness begins. Christ, on the other hand, always knows how and what to pray.

Thank Him for being your great High Priest. He lives to interrupt your life with power.

Praise

....

....

....

....

....

Repentance

....

....

....

....

....

Acknowledgment

....

....

....

....

....

Intercession

....

....

....

....

....

Supplication for Self

....

....

....

....

....

Equipping

....

....

....

....

....

NICHOLAS PAVLOFF

Day Thirty-Nine

*"I loathe my very life; therefore I will give free rein to my complaint
and speak out in the bitterness of my soul" (Job 10:1).*

Scripture Reading: Job 10:1-2; Proverbs 14:10; 18:7

People who loathe their very lives can be difficult to bear. The words of Job shed some light on what motivates their self-hatred. Those who hate their own lives often exhibit the following behaviors:

They **"give free rein to [their] complaints."** People who loathe their own lives often complain constantly. No one can do anything right. Nothing suits nor satisfies. If you are the object of someone's constant complaints, no matter how you've tried, God's Word says something important for you—the problem isn't that you can't do anything right. The problem is the complainer's tragic estimation that everything in his or her life is wrong.

They **"speak out in the bitterness"** of their souls. This specific sign exceeds complaining and proceeds to cutting. Many of us have been deeply wounded by words flowing from the bitterness of another person's soul. We've destructively rehearsed the cutting words repeatedly in our minds, allowing them to scar us almost irreparably.

What can you do? Perhaps wonderful healing could begin if you recognize the cause of constant complaining and cutting words. If you are the object of someone's ongoing meanness, you are not the problem. Job 10:1 illustrates how people who exhibit these two behaviors are suffering from a deep self-loathing.

Start praying diligently for the person's release. They are in horrible bondage. Ask God to flood you with mercy. When you must be in their presence, ask Him to fill you with His Spirit. Through a supernatural empowerment only God can give, use gentle answers to turn away wrath (see Prov. 15:1). If you are in the person's frequent or constant company, seek sound counsel. You may need to work with a Christian counselor or support group to learn to deal with the situation.

As we pray for those who have injured us with esteem-damaging complaints and bitter words, let's not forget to pray for ourselves. We may develop some negative behaviors as a result of this situation.

Self loathing can be contagious. Let's allow God to shed some light on our lives. Are we giving "free rein" to our complaints? Would others characterize us as complainers? Do we feel justified in constantly airing our negative opinions? Are we virtually impossible to please? Are we speaking out in bitterness of soul? Sooner or later if we're harboring bitterness, it will bubble to the surface. Let's allow God to bring healing to us even if the other person never changes.

We only have one life on earth to live. Let's not live it in loathing. A growing relationship with Christ is the cure. His is a life we can love.

Praise

....

....

....

....

....

Repentance

....

....

....

....

....

Acknowledgment

....

....

....

....

....

Intercession

....

....

....

....

....

Supplication for Self

....

....

....

....

....

Equipping

....

....

....

....

....

Day Forty

"When the trumpets sounded, the people shouted, and at the sound of the trumpet, when the people gave a loud shout, the wall collapsed; so every man charged straight in, and they took the city" (Josh. 6:20).

Scripture Reading: Joshua 6:1-20

Some years ago, a newspaper ran an article entitled, "The Walls of Jericho Really Did Come Tumbling Down." Imagine that. God always does what He says, but sometimes He gives conditional promises: "if you will—then I will." Such was the case in Jericho. God said, "See, I have delivered Jericho into your hands, along with its king and its fighting men." Joshua must have looked at that imposing city with its impenetrable wall and thought, *It doesn't look like mine to me!* God's message was: "The victory is already yours, but I want you to do a few things to take it!"

God often directs us in similar ways. In the battles we face victory is already ours by position, but victory may never be ours by possession if He gets no cooperation. God has overcome our every enemy by the blood of the Lamb, Jesus Christ. But some victories are ours, not just to have but to take. Here are a few biblical suggestions for possessing the victories that are ours because of Christ:

1. Stay armed for battle (see v. 3,9). These men were armed with swords, not guns. The Word is our sword (see Eph. 6:17). We'll never possess our victories without it.

2. Stay on course (see v. 3,14). Continue to "march" in the center of God's will. Don't give up. Don't lose hope. The battle is the Lord's and He will be faithful. He will not only give you the victory if you remain faithful, but He also won't waste a moment of the battle.

3. Stick close to your battalion (see v. 13). March closely to fellow overcomers—those dedicated to living in victory. We win very few battles disconnected from other victors in Christ. Remember, not everyone in Christ is pursuing victory. Be careful not to surround yourself solely with victims.

4. Stay alert (see v. 18). Aggressively avoid things you know will be your own destruction. Most of the time we are well aware of our potential pitfalls. The enemy often wraps temptations in appetizing, colorful, or sensuous packages, "but keep away" (see v. 18) for your own good!

These steps are not easy, but the victorious life is worth the work. Do you suppose Joshua and the Israelites preferred to stay home and read about the crumbled wall in the *Canaan Chronicle*? Or, do you think they were astounded and privileged to participate and observe God at work firsthand? We want to be smack in the middle of God's victories. No way to do that without being smack in the middle of the battlefield.

Want a little extra motivation? These steps don't just lead to victory. Each step represents a victory of its own! Until the big one—hang in there. Victory is coming!

Praise

....

....

....

....

....

....

Repentance

....

....

....

....

....

Acknowledgment

....

....

....

....

....

Intercession

....

....

....

....

....

Supplication for Self

....

....

....

....

....

Equipping

....

....

....

....

....

J.D. MARSTON

Day Forty-One

"But Jehu took no heed to walk in the law of the Lord God of Israel with all his heart: for he departed not from the sins of Jeroboam" (2 Kings 10:31, KJV).

Scripture Reading: 2 Kings 10:12-31

These few brief verses reveal some of Scripture's most interesting characters. Allow me to introduce you to Jehu, one of the bloodiest kings ever to reign over Israel—and one of the most effective. Take another look at verses 28 and 29. Jehu single-handedly destroyed Baal worship in Israel, but the next word is one we don't want dangling on the ends of our spiritual service records: HOWEVER. Jehu's was a pretty serious "however." Read it again: "However, he did not turn away from the sins of Jeroboam...the worship of the golden calves at Bethel and Dan" (v. 29).

What went wrong? Jehu was a successful king! He was an authentic Old Testament super-hero! The enemy of evil! The rival of wrong! But he crashed spiritually.

We can learn a crucial lesson from Jehu's example. These verses reveal exactly what went wrong in his life, and we're all at risk. Look again at his chariot ride with Jehonadab in verses 15-16. In all likelihood Jehonadab was a reluctant passenger. No one wanted to hitch a ride with Jehu. 2 Kings 9:20 says his driving was "like a madman." Jehu was the ancients' answer to Speed Racer. This man had bugs in his teeth. Poor Jehonadab. We never hear of him after 2 Kings 10. He may have been confined to a home for the scared-half-to-death.

Jehu had a serious character flaw. He was an adrenaline freak. He was happy and effective as long as life was flooding with excitement! But the day-to-day task of living faithfully? The Bible wraps up his spiritual service record with a tragic ribbon: "Jehu took no heed to walk in the law of the Lord God of Israel with all his heart."

You see, Jehu could run but he couldn't walk. None of us are exempt from falling in this trap. We crave excitement—the best worship service, the most charismatic speakers. We tend to be most passionate about God when He is working wonders. We plead for revival—not always for the purest reasons—sometimes just for the excitement. Sometimes we want the God of the most high, not the Most High God.

Micah 6:8 says: "He has showed you, O man, what is good. And what does the Lord require of you? To act justly and to love mercy and to walk humbly with your God." God is looking for folks who just want to walk with Him—in the quiet as well as the crisis. Because, you see, that's where the excitement is—in having a daily, intimate relationship with the Creator of the universe.

The folks who walk with God in the "daily-ness" of life won't have to worry about a tacky "however" dangling on the end of their spiritual service record—nor those nasty bugs in their teeth.

Praise

....

....

....

....

....

....

Repentance

....

....

....

....

....

Acknowledgment

....

....

....

....

....

Intercession

....

....

....

....

....

Supplication for Self

....

....

....

....

....

Equipping

....

....

....

....

....

Day Forty-Two

"'You don't know what you are asking,' Jesus said to them" (Matt. 20:22).

Scripture Reading: Matthew 20:20-28

In our quest to become effective prayer warriors, we need to know God's heart. As we become more aware of His priorities and objectives, we begin to understand a little more how He thinks; therefore, we are better equipped to pray in His will.

At first glance, the mother of James and John seemed to have unmitigated gall in her request. In reality she came to Christ in humility (see v. 20). She knelt before Him and made a request. This was not a disrespectful woman; she was a dedicated mother who wanted only the best for her sons. In her faith she believed that Christ's kingdom was imminent, and she wanted her sons on each side of His throne.

Christ responded, "You don't know what you are asking." (If He granted her request, one of her boys was going to be sitting on God's lap—since Christ sits to the Father's right.) One of the most compassionate actions Jesus ever takes is to overrule a prayer request when we don't know what we're asking. Christ knew a guarantee of grandeur would do nothing positive for James or John, but a life of selfless servant-hood would guarantee them grandeur in the kingdom.

We want great things for those we love. We want only the best for them, but we sometimes don't realize that what we're asking may not be best. We want them to "arrive" in life. Christ wants them on the way.

God often convicts me about things I request for my loved ones. Through my journal He pointed out my many requests for my daughters to avoid trials. Invariably my next prayer would be, "make them mighty women of God." I could almost hear Him saying, "Beth, make up your mind." His words from 1 Peter 1:7 pierced my heart: Trials "come so that your faith…may be proved genuine and may result in praise, glory and honor when Jesus Christ is revealed." More than anything I want my girls' lives to prove genuine and to honor God. I'm learning now to pray that He simply be as gentle as possible as He continues working His glory in them.

I asked God to let my mother avoid all suffering in her struggle with cancer. Then His words struck me to the core: "I am coming soon. Hold on to what you have, so that no one will take your crown" (Rev. 3:11). I realized that I may have been inadvertently interfering with her crowns. God may have been preparing the "crown of life" for her, given to those who remain faithful through suffering (Jas. 1:12).

I prayed for God to raise up a husband for a friend. Then I watched her develop a relationship with God and a personal ministry that required single-minded devotion.

No, we don't always know what we're asking. We must continue to learn what He values. Then as we pray, allow the great High Priest to overrule when our requests for those we love would cheat them of God's best.

Praise

....

....

....

....

....

....

Repentance

....

....

....

....

....

Acknowledgment

....

....

....

....

....

Intercession

....

....

....

....

....

Supplication for Self

....

....

....

....

....

Equipping

....

....

....

....

....

NICHOLAS PAVLOFF

Day Forty-Three

"Hear us, O our God, for we are despised. Turn their insults back on their own heads. Give them over as plunder in a land of captivity" (Neh. 4:4).

Scripture Reading: Nehemiah 4:1-6

The enemy will do virtually anything to steal our focus as we serve Christ. In his attempts, he often sends something more powerful than an outbreak of boils. He sends criticism, and he never lacks a willing vessel. The world is filled with amateur critics. Satan just instructs them to do what comes naturally.

God appointed Nehemiah to lead the Jews in rebuilding the wall of Jerusalem. At the first sign of success, critics raised their ugly heads. Their criticism came in the form of ridicule. Nothing makes you want to quit as much as feeling stupid. The enemy preyed on their hidden fears that the task might be too much for them.

Have you ever been there? I have! The moment someone spoke my fears, my heart nearly melted. Soon I thought the task was never God's idea in the first place. Many times I might have given up in despair, but God kept reconfirming His will.

If we successfully accomplish our God-given tasks, we must learn to deal with criticism. Nehemiah was a wise man. He knew exactly how to deal with his critics. He told God about them. Look at his words. You even have my permission to grin a little.

Nehemiah went straight to God and said things like, "Turn their insults back on their own heads." We said the same sort of things when we were kids—we just used a little different terminology: "Same to you but more of it!"

Nehemiah didn't direct his statements to his critics, however. He shared his feelings with God. He poured out his heart until he felt better. The result? "So we rebuilt the wall till all of it reached half its height, for the people worked with all their heart."

The enemy's attempt to steal our focus is actually an attempt to remove our hearts from our God-given tasks. The center of our focus fills our hearts. If we're focused on criticism and the subsequent feelings of bitterness and inferiority, our hearts will give up the task. Our effectiveness will suffer terribly. Today's Bible example offers a new defense to Satan's better-than-boils strategy. I call the defense "operation tattletale."

When you're working with all your heart to accomplish God's will and the enemy throws criticism your way, take it to God immediately. He will take up your cause and return your heart and your focus to the task.

A last thought. Is all criticism from Satan? Unfortunately no. How can we know whether or not a criticism is from the enemy? Satan is the father of lies. His criticism will be untrue. If the criticism fits, DON'T QUIT! Just readjust. (I've been there, too.) If you know God has called you to the task, you may be laying the right bricks—but at the wrong angle. God won't leave us stranded with an arm load of bricks. Go ahead and unload—then get your heart back in your task.

Praise

....

....

....

....

....

Repentance

....

....

....

....

....

Acknowledgment

....

....

....

....

....

Intercession

....

....

....

....

....

....

Supplication for Self

....

....

....

....

....

....

Equipping

....

....

....

....

....

Day Forty-Four

"The secret things belong to the Lord our God, but the things revealed belong to us and to our children forever, that we may follow all the words of this law" (Deut. 29:29).

Scripture Reading: Deuteronomy 29:29–30:4

Beloved, as you hold your Bible in your hands, you hold "the things revealed." You possess all the information you can handle, right in front of you, from the omniscient mind of God. But He has so much more, so much we do not know, secret things known only to the Creator of the universe.

Secrets make us uncomfortable, don't they? Especially if we're not in on them. It could be enough to drive a person crazy unless the secret keeper is someone we trust. Yes, God is keeping secrets, but we can find great comfort in at least three assurances.

The secret things of God cannot be contrary to His character. His secrets are just like He is: merciful, loving, just, righteous, wonderful, and good. In His fairness, God made His requirements and judgments known; therefore, the secret things are glorious things. We need not fear His unknowns. God does not have a dark side for "God is light; in him there is no darkness at all" (1 John 1:5).

Can you think of a time when you thought God was unjust? Do you view the situation differently now? How has the passage of time changed your perspective?

The secret things are too much for us. If He withholds information from us, it is because we cannot comprehend the information in our present form. Christ knew all things that were to come upon Him; He knew the secret things. Yes, He could see the suffering in advance, but He also could envision the ultimate glory. So "for the joy set before Him," He endured (Heb.12:2). Knowing our plans in advance would be too much for us. Our human vision is so desperately nearsighted, we would never be able to see the glory for the pain.

Have you been through an experience you thought you could never endure? Did walking through the valley increase or decrease your faith? Can you think of any reasons why God chose not to show you in advance what you were about to experience?

The secret things are a surprise. One day we will "know fully" even as we are "fully known" (1 Cor. 13:12). We have the ultimate surprise party coming and God isn't about to give it away. Until then He grants an occasional hint—like the sight of a majestic mountain that suggests, "If this is earth, what indeed must heaven be like?"

We don't need to feel spiritually immature because of how little we understand. We can be encouraged by knowing that anything beyond us falls in the category of glorious and wonderful. Until God shares His secrets, we hold enough in our hands to keep us challenged—we hold God's Word.

Our Savior is the Keeper of all knowledge—the Omniscient One. Whatever is beyond the pages of Scripture, Beloved, is simply too wonderful for us to know.

Praise

....

....

....

....

....

Repentance

....

....

....

....

....

Acknowledgment

....

....

....

....

....

Intercession

....

....

....

....

....

....

Supplication for Self

....

....

....

....

....

Equipping

....

....

....

....

....

NICHOLAS PAVLOFF

Day Forty-Five

"Jesus said to them, 'My Father is always at his work to this very day, and I, too, am working'" (John 5:17).

Scripture Reading: John 5:16-19

I've learned a few hard lessons about using words like *always* and *never* when exercising the audacity to speak for God. From time to time someone asks me, "Do you think God can...?" I would hate for you to know how I've answered some of those questions in the past. My own hard head has made a liar out of me more than once.

I've come to this conclusion: God can do anything He wants if it's not contrary to His will or His Word. He is able. Whether or not He chooses to do a particular thing is His business, but His ability is certain.

An absolutist by heart, I am relieved to know I can still safely apply a few "always" and "nevers"—those labeled by God Himself. Today we get to grab hold of an "always." Jesus assures us, "My Father is always at his work to this very day and I, too, am working." No matter what is happening in your life or mine or the chaotic world around us, we can rest on at least one "always." GOD IS AT WORK.

Whether or not you see a hint of Him, you can "always" count on Him. He has not given up or over. God is gloriously stubborn.

Christians receive an added bonus. Philippians 1:6 says, "He who began a good work in you will carry it on to completion." Not only can you be assured God is at work, but you can also be assured that the work involving you is good and He is committed to completing it.

The word *good* is important. A few synonyms for the original word *agathos* are "profitable, excellent, distinguished."[11]

Beloved, the only time God is working against you is when you are working against yourself. He desires to work to your profit, to your excellence, to your sanctification as a set-apart, distinguished person of faith.

If your works are ultimately self-destructive, He's working against them. Once we belong to Him, He obligates Himself to the good work. He works "for us" even when we vote against Him...and thus erupts the war of the works. He's too jealous for your good to let you win, so why not give in? He is always at His work—completing what He started.

God's not just up to something good. He's up to something excellent.

Praise

....

....

....

....

....

Repentance

....

....

....

....

....

Acknowledgment

....

....

....

....

....

Intercession

....

....

....

....

....

Supplication for Self

....

....

....

....

....

Equipping

....

....

....

....

....

Day Forty-Six

"Do not test the Lord your God" (Deut. 6:16).

Scripture Reading: Deuteronomy 6:10-19; Luke 4:9-12

In both the Old and New Testaments, Scripture firmly warns us not to put God to the test. We may be unknowingly offending the heart of God because we do not understand the meaning of the commandment. The meaning of the word *test,* regarding our actions toward God, is similar in both Testaments.

The Greek word used in the New Testament is *ekpeirazo.* It means "refusing to believe Him or His Word until He has manifested His power."[12] Faith is the opposite of putting God to a test. The essence of faith is believing God prior to "proof." Testing is demanding proof or a manifestation of the Spirit prior to belief.

Not coincidentally, each time Scripture forbids testing God, the commandment is directed toward His own people. Do you see why God is so offended by being tested? He has proven Himself faithful. If we've known Him long, who among us could claim God has not faithfully revealed Himself in many ways? So when we ask Him to keep proving what He has already revealed, we both test and insult Him.

God our Father is a giver by nature. He grants us full permission to make our petitions known, but He also asks that we check our motives (Jas. 4:3). If our motive is to see proof, according to Scripture we're testing God.

Our attempts to test God take many forms, but let me cite one fairly common example from people who would never knowingly offend God. A precious believer said to me recently, "Beth, I really want to receive the gift of tongues and I wonder how you feel about it."

I responded that in matters of God and His Word, opinions mean absolutely nothing—but I did pose a question. "Why do you desire this particular gift?"

I could tell she was truly thinking about the question. I sensed the direct leadership of the Holy Spirit to continue. "Is it because you feel this gift would help you to more effectively edify the body of Christ, or is there any possibility you want a physical manifestation of the Spirit for further proof God exists and has chosen you?"

The question applies to many other situations as well. Have you ever asked God to act, not for His glory but to settle your doubts? Think of some possible examples.

As we grow in Christ, let's not only be more cautious about the things we ask but also about our motives. Do we ask for a miracle to increase our ability to bring God glory, or do we want proof He exists and loves us? Food for thought.

Today let's thank Him for the many ways He has proven Himself in our lives apart from our demands. Let's ask Him to make us people who do not put Him to the test.

Great is His faithfulness!

Praise

....
....
....
....
....
....

Repentance

....
....
....
....
....

Acknowledgment

....
....
....
....
....

Intercession

....

....

....

....

....

....

Supplication or Self

....

....

....

....

....

Equipping

....

....

....

....

....

NICHOLAS PAVLOFF

Day Forty-Seven

*"But our citizenship is in heaven. And we eagerly await a Savior
from there, the Lord Jesus Christ" (Phil. 3:20).*

Scripture Reading: Philippians 3:18-21; John 14:1-4

Most of the time life on earth has to get pretty miserable for us to long for our heavenly home. Don't you agree? We're just not homesick most of the time. In many ways we are less than excited about what awaits us.

My longing for heaven is actually my longing for Christ. I want to spend eternity in heaven because He is there and I have loved Him since childhood. I yearn to see His face. I can't wait to worship Him in person, talk with Him, and take a walk with Him.

In the past I was quite excited about spending eternity with Christ but less enthused about the setting. I simply couldn't picture a perfect place. Heaven seemed like a dreamland to me. Aspects of this earth really appeal to me. Rugged mountains and rapid rivers. The distant sound of a train. Old wooden bridges. Small country churches with pealing paint and off-key pianos. Toothless first graders.

I want Christ so intensely I can hardly bear it, but I realize at times that I want Him here—near the things I love. Then the greater reality hits: He wants you and me there—near the things He loves.

Our problem with heaven is fear of trading in the familiar for the ethereal. We picture our future home like a vaporous ghost town where we'll have see-through bodies and sing for eons. Let's allow God to readjust our thinking. Heaven is authentic real estate. We'll feel ground beneath our feet. We will have touchable bodies. Contrary to popular belief, we will not be angels. We will be completed, perfected, suddenly immortal human beings. The objects surrounding us will be tangible. Heaven is a place of clarity and complete reality. We will recognize one another and fellowship together. We will live in an active community. We will experience the indescribable joy of true worship and the ultimate in emotional and spiritual intimacy.

What we enjoy most on earth will be greatly enhanced in heaven. The best of earth is only a shadow of what is to come. We will give up nothing good. Good will simply be perfected. Christ said, "I am going there to prepare a place for you" (John 14:2). He is preparing a "home" for us in every sense of the word—not a place where we'll feel like strangers. In heaven we will exchange longing for belonging. We will sit, stand, walk, eat, touch, and express emotions. Our senses will be quickened in ways that would be unbearable in our present form. The veil of the fathomable will be removed from our eyes. We will behold reality.

The best part of heaven is that Christ will be there. He waits to show us our new homes, new neighbors, the best of everything we've loved—only so much better. "Our citizenship is in heaven." Walk in faith toward a better reality.

Praise

....

....

....

....

....

Repentance

....

....

....

....

....

Acknowledgment

....

....

....

....

....

Intercession

....

....

....

....

....

....

Supplication for Self

....

....

....

....

....

Equipping

....

....

....

....

....

Day Forty-Eight

*"After the Lord had said these things to Job, he said to Eliphaz the Temanite,
'I am angry with you and your two friends, because you have not spoken
of me what is right, as my servant Job has'" (Job 42:7).*

Scripture Reading: Job 42:1-9

As we gaze into this pool of Scripture, two truths float to the top. First, God honors honesty. Even though God felt the need to deliver Job a lengthy dissertation on His sovereignty (chapters 38-41), He venerated His servant's honesty. Job responded appropriately to his loss and suffering. He poured out his heart without dishonoring God. He came clean with his confusion and despair.

Job's friends stood before God in marked contrast. They presumed to answer for God. They had the audacity to point out to Job why such suffering had fallen upon him. In reality they didn't know the answer, but they felt compelled to offer explanations. Because they knew so little, they said so much. They spoke as authorities on God and they were wrong. We often fight the same compelling human nature when someone is going through suffering. We try to figure out why. We secretly wonder if we don't know something. We offer our theories—sometimes as presumptuous facts.

Answering for the Ruler of the universe is a frightful thing. How much safer to simply say, "I don't know why this is happening to you, but I do know God loves you." God honors honesty over pious platitudes. A wise man admits to his ignorance. An ignorant man pretends he is wise.

A second truth emerges from today's text: God's anger doesn't mean the end. Even in God's anger with Job's counselors, He was merciful. Though they were brazen and spoke for God, He did not cast them away. I love God's frankness with Eliphaz in verse 7: "I am angry with you and your two friends." Many of us have mistakenly concluded that if someone is angry with us, they cannot love us. Thus, we fail to deal with our anger in ways that honor God and build up people. We need to learn the meaning of "be ye angry, and sin not" (Eph. 4:26, KJV).

Can you recall a time when you have been angry at someone you love? Did you express your anger in an honest way? Did you express your anger in an unloving way? Or, did you suppress your anger? I find great comfort in knowing God is fully willing to tell us when He is angry—AND WHY!

God explained His anger to Eliphaz, "Because you have not spoken of me what is right." God may not speak audibly from heaven today, but He is perfectly capable of telling us through the conviction of His Holy Spirit when He is angry or grieved.

We incite God's anger when we answer for Him inappropriately; yet even in such a presumptuous infraction, God extends mercy. "Because of the Lord's great love we are not consumed, for his compassions never fail" (Lam. 3:21).

Praise

....

....

....

....

....

....

Repentance

....

....

....

....

....

Acknowledgment

....

....

....

....

....

Intercession

....

....

....

....

....

....

Supplication for Self

....

....

....

....

....

Equipping

....

....

....

....

....

NICHOLAS PAVLOFF

Day Forty-Nine

"After Job had prayed for his friends, the Lord made him prosperous again and gave him twice as much as he had before" (Job 42:10).

Scripture Reading: Job 42:10-17

Ours is a God of restoration. Do not confuse restoration with replacement. God's way is not just to replace what we've lost but to restore us.

When we have experienced a devastating loss, His aim is not simply to put something in its place. His aim is to minister to the hurting soul. If I lose a child, I might be helped by receiving another child—but I am not healed. Our infinitely wise God does far more than replace. He goes straight to the heart to heal.

The Scripture passage demonstrates that God was after Job's innermost healing and restoration because He involved Job in the process of forgiving the errant counselors. Job had been badly injured by several of his best friends. Without God's intervention Job would long remember their hurtful words and misplaced blame. He might have had the dignity to continue the external expressions of friendship, but he would have battled resentment for the rest of his life.

Yes, God could have replaced Job's friends with others, but a simple replacement would never have accomplished restoration. Job's bitterness would have remained. Instead, God began mending Job's heart through prayer.

The Scripture does not record the exact dialogue between God and His servant Job, but at some point the Lord instructed him to pray for the friends who had so badly wounded him.

Remembering Job's ability to be honest, can you imagine what his first response might have been? If Job were like us, his first requests were probably things he prayed for God to do *to* his friends rather than *for* them! But prayer is so healing. I've often said that God has to be God because only He could totally change a stubborn human heart like mine in a few minutes of honest prayer.

In Matthew 5:44 Christ said, "But I tell you: Love your enemies and pray for those who persecute you, that you may be sons of your Father in heaven." Do you see it? Prayer for those who have hurt us is not just for their sakes, it's for OURS! Perhaps a far greater work is accomplished in us.

Remember, beloved one, God is not just trying to replace something you've lost. He's trying to reach your heart and heal you, but He requires your cooperation. If you are willing to get down on your knees and let God begin His glorious work of restoration through prayer, He will faithfully bless "the latter part" of your life "more than the first." Can you imagine that?

Thank goodness God is not limited by our imaginations!

Praise

....

....

....

....

....

....

Repentance

....

....

....

....

....

Acknowledgment

....

....

....

....

....

Intercession

....

....

....

....

....

Supplication for Self

....

....

....

....

....

Equipping

....

....

....

....

....

Day Fifty

*"Since you are my rock and my fortress,
for the sake of your name lead and guide me"* (Ps. 31:3).

Scripture Reading: Psalm 31:1-8

Life is hard. Always has been—but people in past generations were usually only aware of hardship in their immediate sphere. Our present society is graced with satellites that daily dump worldwide disasters in our living rooms. Good still exists out there somewhere but, let's face it, it's not news. Daily doses of the world's meanness, violence, and depravity take their toll.

One natural result of constant contact with negative influence is a hard heart. In reality our hardness of heart is nothing more than a fortress we've constructed around a frightened heart. We build layer upon layer of protection to prevent being hurt. Tragically, the same fortress that won't allow the hurt in—also won't let the love out. Our fortress of self-protection becomes our prison.

Whether or not we realize it, we spend untold effort in attempts to avoid pain. Yes, even Christians. Do you journal your prayers? If so, check it out. Notice how often you've asked God to deliver you or someone you know or love from pain.

I'm not suggesting that we can't or shouldn't ask God to deliver us from pain. We have biblical permission by Christ's example in Matthew 26:36-44 and Paul's example in 2 Corinthians 12:8 to ask Him to remove any thorn (or cup).

I am suggesting, however, that we adopt a new, eye-opening perspective—the goal of life is not the absence of pain. It is the presence of God and the glory of God. When He can work glory without pain, He does. When He can't, it's going to hurt. But it's also going to be worth it someday (see Rom. 8:18).

Abundant living is impossible behind the walls of our self-constructed fortresses. Anything we've done to protect ourselves will work to imprison us. If we don't risk our hearts, we deny ourselves some of life's richest experiences.

I'm certainly not proposing a life without protection, but only one way exists to find PROTECTION without IMPRISONMENT. We must make God our Fortress. Only God can hem you in from every side, yet "set your feet in a spacious place." It's only in His protection that we remain free.

After the Oklahoma City bombing, Garth Brooks, an OKC native, wrote a song with this basic message: It's not that I think I can change this world; but I will not let this world change me. He sang a very biblical message (see Rom. 12:2).

Let's not grow cold with this world. Let's risk it. If it hurts, we won't break. If we're in Christ, we're not nearly as fragile as we may believe. It's time to let God cut away all the layers we've built around our hearts (see Deut. 30:6).

Christ is your Fortress—your protection. Go ahead—live a little!

Praise

....

....

....

....

....

....

Repentance

....

....

....

....

....

Acknowledgment

....

....

....

....

....

Intercession

....

....

....

....

....

Supplication for Self

....

....

....

....

....

Equipping

....

....

....

....

....

NICHOLAS PAVLOFF

Day Fifty-One

"Immediately Jesus made the disciples get into the boat and go on ahead of him to the other side, while he dismissed the crowd" (Matt. 14:22).

Scripture Reading: Matthew 14:22-33

We can be smack in the center of God's will and still go through terrible storms. Christ loved the disciples with all His heart, yet He "made" them get into the boat when He knew a storm was coming. They were exactly where they were supposed to be and still experienced frightening turbulence.

Can you relate to the disciples? Have you experienced a time when you knew you were where God wanted you to be, but the storms were overwhelming?

Not all the storms in life result from either sin or warfare. Some occur like clockwork to purposely rock our boats. However, if Christ has appointed our place in the storm, you can be sure He purposes a show. But, we must be looking past our own boat to see Him.

One of my family's worst storms occurred when Michael, the child we raised for seven years, left our home to return to his birth mother. We received countless cards and letters which were a great comfort to us. Many of them attributed our loss to Satan and our storm to spiritual warfare. We understood the assumption because it was clearly the easiest explanation—albeit not necessarily an accurate one.

I am so thankful God was clear in His message to us during those days. We knew without a shadow of a doubt that Michael's return to his birth mother was the expressed will of God. We had no idea why nor do we have many answers now, but we were certain God was directing the events.

Christ calls us to walk by faith through our storms. It seems like a big requirement until we realize Christ does far more than that—He walks on the water during our storms. God has placed all things under Christ's feet—including the waves that break relentlessly against us. He is in charge. He is right there.

Please don't miss an important element in this story: Christ walked on the water before He calmed the storm. If He had simply calmed the storm, the disciples would have missed His majesty. And what a shame. His majesty was the whole point.

We want Christ to hurry and calm the storm. He wants us to find Him in the midst of it first.

Praise

....

....

....

....

....

....

Repentance

....

....

....

....

....

Acknowledgment

....

....

....

....

....

Intercession

....

....

....

....

....

Supplication for Self

....

....

....

....

....

Equipping

....

....

....

....

....

Day Fifty-Two

"But solid food is for the mature, who by constant use
have trained themselves to distinguish good from evil" (Heb. 5:14).

Scripture Reading: Hebrews 5:11-14

Nothing is more appropriate for an infant than milk. Often we overwhelm infants in Christ by shoving them down the cafeteria line while they are still trying to digest a carton of milk. Today's text in no way rushes the babe in Christ. The writer referred to the opposite problem. Many believers who years ago received Christ are still eating Cheerios and choosing to stay in nursery school.

To imagine why Christians remain infants isn't so difficult. When I was little, I hated promotion Sunday at church. I was comfortable in my class. I understood the schedule. I was accustomed to my teacher. I liked the cookies and the other kids in my class. I never liked promoting to the next grade—but no one gave me a choice.

Once a beloved teacher explained promotion to a room of quivering-lipped kindergartners. She said: "I used to feel just like you. I never wanted to leave my teacher or my classroom. Then I thought how silly I would look one day all grown-up in one of these little bitty chairs." She was a beautifully round little lady who, to make the children laugh, squatted down on one of the tiny chairs. The legs gave way as she toppled to the floor. It worked. They laughed and the fear dissipated.

The Hebrews writer described a similar scene. Believers who should have been ready to lead, train others, and assume the responsibilities of mature Christians were still squeezing their considerable weight into nursery-school chairs.

Our churches are experiencing a leadership crisis though our membership roles are full. Many of us reached our comfort level long ago and refuse to move on. "Enough," we say to ourselves, "No sense in being eaten up with this thing." No one forces us to promote to the next level in Christianity. We can stay in those chairs and complain about the lack of qualified leadership, or we can confess our reluctance to move toward maturity and accept the challenge of promotions for the rest of our lives.

As I think back on childhood days in Sunday School, I feel pretty old. Yet I'd never go back even if I could. Life was easier then—but it certainly wasn't better. Less responsibility—but no clue about fulfillment. I like my life much better as a grown-up.

Sometimes we have to let a little cooperation displace some comfort. How can you and I prepare ourselves for promotions? By training ourselves through the constant use of God's Word. It's an amazing book, isn't it? A primer for the babe in Christ. A dictionary to the adolescent. A world book to the scholar. Milk for some. Meat for others. That's your textbook—and your ticket to the next level.

Is it time to move on? How long has it been since you were stretched and challenged and forced out of your routine? Perhaps it's time to promote.

Praise

....

....

....

....

....

....

Repentance

....

....

....

....

....

Acknowledgment

....

....

....

....

....

Intercession

....

....

....

....

....

Supplication for Self

....

....

....

....

....

Equipping

....

....

....

....

J.D. MARSTON

Day Fifty-Three

"For no matter how many promises God has made, they are 'Yes' in Christ. And so through him the 'Amen' is spoken by us to the glory of God'" (2 Cor. 1:20).

Scripture Reading: 2 Corinthians 1:12-22

As believers in Christ, let's ask ourselves a tough question: Do those who know us characterize us most by the things we do not do because of our belief—or by the things we do?

Clearly, what we don't do is important. The Ten Commandments consist almost entirely of "shalt nots." Without a doubt, certain "don'ts" must characterize our lives if we are seeking to please God. But are the "don'ts" all that distinguish us as followers of Christ? Does our personal brand of Christianity lend negative connotations?

I believe Christians who are known only by the things they don't do are helping to lend Christianity a bad name. Consider the office environment. Are we doing our jobs as Christians in a secular workplace if no one there can stand to be around us? If we repel people, perhaps we've allowed ourselves to be characterized by all the things we do not do—unknowingly branding ourselves and Christianity with a "no" mentality.

God's Word tells us that Christ is the "yes" of God! After all the negatives of the Old Testament "Law," after rivers of sacrifices that could never atone for sin, and after every good intention toward perfection fell miserably short of the glory of God, the Father sent His one and only Son. Through the cross, He said, "Yes!"

So if we're still characterizing God primarily by His negatives rather than His affirmatives, our "religion" needs an update! Am I suggesting God no longer says, "No"? Not on your life. But I am convinced that even His "no's" are doors He closes along our corridors to lead us to the "yes."

For example, God says "no" to premarital sex so He can say "yes" to a blessed physical union reserved for husband and wife. He also says "no" to one job or position because He has chosen to say "yes" to one further down the corridor and better suited to His plan. In Christ, God wants to be characterized as a "yes" kind of God. He says "yes" to joy even in difficult circumstances, to wealth even in poverty, to strength even in weakness. You see, when we say "no" to the cravings of our flesh, God says "yes" to the abundant filling of His Spirit.

Likewise, God wants us to be characterized most by the things we do rather than those we don't. He wants others to see the "yes" of Christ in us—that we are a people of positive action, that we perform our jobs with excellence, enhance a friendly environment, love the unlovely, forgive the transgressor, help the oppressed, lend a listening ear, love an invisible God, and make others want to love Him, too.

Now that's the kind of Christian that makes others want to say "yes" to Christ. That's positive. That's action.

Praise

....

....

....

....

....

Repentance

....

....

....

....

....

Acknowledgment

....

....

....

....

....

Intercession

....

....

....

....

....

....

Supplication for Self

....

....

....

....

....

Equipping

....

....

....

....

....

Day Fifty-Four

"Let another praise you, and not your own mouth; someone else,
and not your own lips" (Prov. 27:2).

Scripture Reading: Proverbs 27:2; Luke 5:27-32 and Matthew 9:9-13

When I was a little girl, I adored *Highlights,* a popular children's magazine. I particularly enjoyed one feature. In every issue two similar cartoon-style pictures appeared. The object of the activity was to discover every missing detail in the second picture. I experienced great satisfaction if I could pinpoint each detail without peeking at the answer. Let's look at two Gospel accounts of Matthew's call to be a disciple as if we're looking at those activity pictures. First, search Luke's version. Then compare it to Matthew's version. List each detail missing in the second "picture."

You may be more adept than I at this game, but I found two details in Luke's Gospel missing in Matthew's account. First Luke tells us Matthew got up, left everything, and followed Jesus. Matthew simply said he got up and followed. The fact that he "left everything," is highly significant. Imagine Christ issuing you the same invitation. What if your livelihood and your relationships were all at risk? Would you "leave everything"? Especially if your "everything" was substantial? Difficult question—yet Luke wanted us to know that's exactly what Matthew did.

A second detail is missing in Matthew's version. He told us Jesus was having dinner at his house. Luke elaborated: "Levi held a great banquet for Jesus at his house." Matthew was a man of considerable wealth. His first reaction on behalf of his new Master was to begin using his resources to the glory of God. Quite impressive.

Interestingly, a third detail differs in the accounts of Matthew and Luke, but this time it appears in Matthew's version and is missing from Luke's. The detail is "mercy." Matthew related a quote from Christ which Luke did not record: "I desire mercy, not sacrifice" (Matt. 9:13).

Matthew knew himself better than Luke or any other human would ever know him. The tax collector was painfully aware of the mercy Christ extended to Him when He said, "Follow me." Matthew immediately became an ambassador of mercy inviting those in need to meet the Divine Mercy-giver personally.

The comparison between Luke and Matthew's version of Matthew's commission reveals a precious balance. Luke was rightfully impressed with Matthew and under the inspiration of the Holy Spirit meticulously revealed the new convert's character. Matthew, on the other hand, was impressed with Christ. He was far too aware of his own frailties to do anything but brag on God's mercy. That's how it should be. "Let another praise you, and not your own mouth; someone else, and not your own lips."

Let's give God freedom to develop in our lives a character impressive to others, but may we never move so far from mercy that we become impressed with ourselves.

Praise

....
....
....
....
....
....

Repentance

....
....
....
....
....

Acknowledgment

....
....
....
....
....

Intercession

....

....

....

....

....

Supplication for Self

....

....

....

....

....

Equipping

....

....

....

....

....

NICHOLAS PAVLOFF

Day Fifty-Five

"Do not withhold good from those who deserve it, when it is in your power to act. Do not say to your neighbor, 'Come back later; I'll give it tomorrow'— when you now have it with you" (Prov. 3:27-28).

Scripture Reading: Proverbs 3:27-35

Often when someone we know is in need, our feelings of inadequacy paralyze us. We know we can't fix the problem, so we remain distant. Our lack of power may keep us from exercising the lesser power we possess. We don't have the power to "fix" lives, but we often have the power to "help" in small but significant ways. Proverbs 3:27-28 teaches us a priceless trait of godliness—timely kindness. Verse 27 instructs us to do good for others when we have the "power to act." Verse 28 tells us to refrain from putting off the good deed when the "neighbor" is in need—today.

Once I overheard a talk-show host encourage her listeners to perform random acts of kindness. God's Word reminds us that we don't have to wait for random opportunities to be kind. Plenty of people we know could use a show of kindness right now.

Because we are aware of so many needy persons, the "plenty" may overwhelm and keep us from extending a timely kindness to one or two. I have a neighbor who is a widow. She is not elderly nor inactive. She works long hours and appears to be very self-sufficient. I watch her drive into her garage and walk into her house alone most every evening. As I've watched her, I've known her greatest need was someone to soothe her loneliness, but the one thing I didn't have was time. The demands of my own family are great. I almost didn't even try to help because I knew I couldn't offer what she really needed.

Then God led me to begin fixing a plate for her any time I prepared more food for dinner than we could eat. I would watch for her to pull into her driveway; then I would run across the street with a hot meal. We have formed a special bond of friendship through a very small act.

I can't fill the emptiness left by her loss, but I can occasionally fill her tummy with something home cooked—and something she didn't have to prepare after a long day of work. I almost missed the blessing because I kept thinking how little I could help. Just because we can't do something great doesn't mean we can't do something good.

In the past I've missed many opportunities because the need was great. God has promised to meet people's needs. We've just been asked to do some good.

Drop a note in someone's mailbox. Leave a message on someone's answering machine. Take someone's preschooler with you while you do errands. Bake a few extra cookies and give them away.

God has more than random acts of kindness for us, Beloved. He has appointments. Let's not miss them just because we can't fix them.

Praise

....
....
....
....
....
....

Repentance

....
....
....
....
....

Acknowledgment

....
....
....
....
....

Intercession

....

....

....

....

....

....

Supplication for Self

....

....

....

....

....

....

Equipping

....

....

....

....

....

Day Fifty-Six

"When Jesus saw his mother there, and the disciple whom he loved standing nearby, he said to his mother, 'Dear woman, here is your son,' and to the disciple, 'Here is your mother'" (John 19:26-27).

Scripture Reading: John 19:17-27

I have often meditated on this tender scene when both a screaming throng and the searing pain of crucifixion momentarily gave way to another concern. In the midst of unimaginable torture, with every breath a struggle, the sight of Jesus' grieving mother and horrified friend captured His attention. Inconceivable compassion spilled from His heart as He bid them to love and support each other.

I see great significance in the fact that He did not minimize their loss or grief. He did not consider their pain an insignificant detail in a work of far greater glory. He did not wonder how they could think so temporally. His heart broke with compassion and He reached out to them in their need.

A glimpse of Christ's heart in this tender moment can be healing for us if we'll let it. You see, He looks on us with the same compassion. Imagine—at the very moment Christ was dying on the cross, salvation was secured for all who would believe. The enemy was defeated. Hell was trembling. Demons were howling. God was momentarily turning His face as every sin known to man was heaped on His Son. The hours Christ spent on the cross represented the most significant moments since time began.

John and Mary's grief and confusion were nothing compared to the awesome work accomplished that afternoon. However, the friend and the mother did not look through eternal eyes to "see" the work of the Savior. They saw the impending loss of someone they loved and wanted nearby. Still, Christ looked upon their suffering and said, "Dear woman, here is your son," and to the disciple, "Here is your mother."

Jesus knew they could not comprehend the greater glory at work. He knew they wanted Him to climb down off the cross and live. For their sakes, He could not suspend His glorious works, yet Christ's heart poured forth compassion.

My friend, at times Christ will do glorious works that involve suffering and loss. He persists in a greater glory even when we kick and scream and beg Him to do otherwise. Why? Because He will not allow us to cheat ourselves of something more marvelous than we can conceive. He knows one day we will understand.

Someday we will celebrate Christ's unwillingness to give in to our demands—even when our begging broke His heart. He is working the greater work. Still, He has overwhelming compassion for our pain and confusion. Christ doesn't grow impatient and wonder how we can be so foolish to hurt over earthly losses. He doesn't even sigh and whisper, "If you only knew." His heart bleeds with mercy and He comes to our aid.

Oh, Beloved, can you trust a heart like His?

Praise

....
....
....
....
....
....

Repentance

....
....
....
....
....

Acknowledgment

....
....
....
....
....

Intercession

....

....

....

....

....

Supplication for Self

....

....

....

....

....

Equipping

....

....

....

....

....

NICHOLAS PAVLOFF

Day Fifty-Seven

"Taste and see that the Lord is good; blessed is the man who takes refuge in him" (Ps. 34:8).

Scripture Reading: Luke 6:27-36; Psalm 34:1-8

On Day fifty-five, we highlighted Proverbs 3:27: "Do not withhold good from those who deserve it, when it is in your power to act." I've purposely waited a few days for those words to sink in before proposing a giant step farther in God's command not to "withhold good"; in fact, it's such a giant step that some of us may be doing the splits. What about doing good to those who don't deserve it?

In Luke 6:27-28 Christ, the glorious Revolutionary, flabbergasted His listeners when He challenged them to take the giant step: "Love your enemies, do good to those who hate you, bless those who curse you, pray for those who mistreat you." He went on to say in Luke 6:33: "If you do good to those who are good to you, what credit is that to you? Even 'sinners' do that." Let's admit it. This command is so Christlike that to obey stretches us completely beyond our natural reach. Following Christ means stepping beyond the norm—into actions only Jesus would take.

No one particularly enjoys doing good to those who treat them badly. So, why should we? I believe three chief reasons exist:

The promise of great reward. God assures us His reward is far beyond the uncomfortable risks we'll be forced to take. Let's be careful not to assume His rewards are always logical (at least to us). We might expect the reward to be winning the favor of the person who hates us. We might even think the reward could come in our privilege to lead the person to faith in Christ. The truth of the matter is they may hate you twice as much after you extend kindness to them. God promises a "great" reward far beyond the logical. You can count on it—but you can't count on what it will be.

The mark of sonship. Once again read Luke 6:35. When we do good to those who hate us, we demonstrate our kinship to our Father, the Most High God because He is "kind to the ungrateful and wicked." We are never more like Christ than when we are willing to stretch beyond our natural likes and dislikes to extend good, love, and mercy to those who despise us.

The taste of God. Psalm 34:8 says, "Taste and see that the Lord is good." Beloved, the Lord is calling us to be appetizers so others will want to taste God! Matthew 10:22 tells us that sometimes people hate us because they hate Christ. When we extend goodness to those who hate us, we give them a taste of the goodness of One far greater. Many will never "taste" God until their appetites have been whetted by the goodness of one of His more palatable ambassadors.

Perhaps you've never thought of yourself as an appetizer before. Let's look at life a little differently today. Our job is to offer people a taste so they will want the main course. Just picture yourself on a cracker—and let Him serve you up with a smile.

Praise

....

....

....

....

....

....

Repentance

....

....

....

....

....

Acknowledgment

....

....

....

....

....

Intercession

....

....

....

....

....

Supplication for Self

....

....

....

....

....

Equipping

....

....

....

....

....

Day Fifty-Eight

"Praise be to the Lord, to God our Savior, who daily bears our burdens" (Ps. 68:19).

Scripture Reading: Psalm 68:1-20

Oh, that we could see the daily-ness of God. Often we picture God so focused on His big plan that we forget how involved in our daily process He desires to be.

Do you really believe and understand how much God wants to be part of your daily life? God is looking for a daily, give-and-take relationship with us, but in this unique relationship He TAKES and He GIVES.

What does God desire to "take" from us daily? According to Psalm 68:19, He intends to take our daily burdens. Are you bearing your own burdens? If so, the load is so unnecessary. Perhaps your heart is in the right place—certainly no one can worry like you because no one loves that person like you. No one understands the circumstances like you. It's complicated. Personal. Secret. Not really God's "field." It's not a religious matter. Anyway, God may not fix this one like we want it. On and on we go until we reason ourselves into burdens too heavy to bear.

Daily—God is willing to take those weights from our weary shoulders. 1 Peter 5:7 says cast "all your care upon him; for he careth for you" (KJV). The invitation applies everyday. He daily "bears our burdens" if we will release our grip on them.

If God takes our burdens daily, what does He give? Lamentations 3:22-23 records one of Scripture's most beautiful promises describing the daily-ness of God: "Because of the Lord's great love we are not consumed, for his compassions never fail. They are new every morning; great is your faithfulness." New every morning—He sees every need in advance. He is acquainted with every burden even before the bad news. Before the sun rises, He metes out His mercy in direct proportion to your day's needs.

God desires to TAKE our burdens and GIVE His mercy. How many times have we carried a burden we could have daily traded in for His mercies? Far too many.

Consider what we do to ourselves. We carry a daily bag of burdens. We add today's to yesterday's until the load is more than we can balance. Finally, it gets so heavy, our backs nearly break and our joy evaporates. We add to the bag until it starts to tear. Sadly, by the time everything spills, we're usually torn apart as well. We feel exhausted, hopeless, and angry at God for not helping. All the while, His hands were outstretched as He whispered through His Word, "Cast them to Me! I care for you!"

God never meant for us to keep heaping burdens in the bag. He wants us to pour them at His feet each day and trade in our burdens for fresh mercies.

I have lots of regrets for past burdens I refused to release—times I made life harder than it had to be. I can't go back and pick up last year's mercies and neither can you, but we can receive today's. Our God is so willing to TAKE AND GIVE. If only we're willing to GIVE AND TAKE.

Praise

....

....

....

....

....

....

Repentance

....

....

....

....

....

Acknowledgment

....

....

....

....

....

Intercession

....

....

....

....

....

....

Supplication for Self

....

....

....

....

....

....

Equipping

....

....

....

....

....

....

NICHOLAS PAVLOFF

Day Fifty-Nine

"Find rest, O my soul, in God alone; my hope comes from him" (Ps. 62:5).

Scripture Reading: Psalm 62

David was not only a deeply spiritual man; he was a deeply emotional man. His psalms are God's glorious concoction of both. David wrote out of great feeling, whether ecstasy, amazement, fear, love, pain, or anger. When he wrote Psalm 62, he dipped his pen deep in the well of disappointment. This is a psalm of dashed expectations. Over and over David trusted people who let him down. No doubt you have, too.

Surely nothing compares to dashed expectations involving a person of God. When a favorite leader falls, we quickly discover how much our relationships with God are feeding off others. The foundation beneath our feet quakes.

When David was scarcely more than a teenager, his eyes were unwillingly pried open by King Saul. He never imagined a man of God could descend to the depths of sin he witnessed in Saul. David later discovered that he too was not immune to sin.

Our church rolls are filled with names of people who no longer darken the doors because someone disappointed them. The infractions vary. It doesn't always take adultery or deceit by a leader. All leaders have to do is fail to live up to expectations.

Dashed expectations can devastate, but something wonderful can come from it—something I'm not sure we can adequately discover any other way. The motivation for Psalm 62 was disappointment—but the theme of David's psalm was GOD ALONE.

Read aloud verses 1-2 and 5-8 and emphasize every repetition of the words *God, He,* or *Him.* Do you hear it? Because he poured out his heart to God, David's experience with shattered expectations did not produce bitterness, it produced a lifelong benediction: God alone. The fifth verse is climactic. "Find rest, O my soul, in God alone; my hope comes from him." Notice the word *hope.* The Hebrew term literally means "a cord, as an attachment." Every one of us is hanging on to something or someone for security. We hold a knotted rope and depend on whatever is on the other end to keep us from falling. Picture that rope in your hands. Then close your eyes and imagine looking up the rope and seeing the other end. Who or what do you see?

As wonderful as that person or possession may be, if it's someone or something other than God alone, you're hanging on by a thread—the wrong thread. You may be "a leaning wall," or a "tottering fence." God alone can hold us up.

GOD ALONE—the next time someone disappoints you, whisper those two words to yourself. If you agree to let that person off the hook and allow only God to grasp the other end of the rope, two things can happen: you'll attach yourself to Someone with an arm strong enough to hold you up; you'll be secure enough to let one arm go free to help the one who disappointed you back to his or her feet.

These kinds of results are worth the painful learning experience. God alone.

Praise

....

....

....

....

....

Repentance

....

....

....

....

....

Acknowledgment

....

....

....

....

....

Intercession

....

....

....

....

....

Supplication for Self

....

....

....

....

....

Equipping

....

....

....

....

....

Day Sixty

"But Mary treasured up all these things and pondered them in her heart" (Luke 2:19).

Scripture Reading: Luke 2:1-20

While they were there, the time came" (Luke 2:6). Time was God's first creation. Genesis 1:1 says, "In the beginning." We could say, "When God first told the clock to tick." From that instant the clock began ticking toward one moment, the birth of Hope—God, clothed in seven pounds of peeling, pink infant flesh. Perfection wrapped in innocence. The first audible sounds from the Logos, Himself, were hungry wails from a set of lungs no bigger than the center of your palm.

Many believed He was the Messiah, but perhaps only one knew beyond a shadow of a doubt. Her name was Mary. She had never "known" a man, yet in her arms she cuddled a son freshly detached from her body. She witnessed the work of God in ways far beyond what is written. Between the lines of Luke Chapter 2 lie incredible experiences. Imagine the first time God crawled. The first time He said, "Mamma." The first time God bumped His head. God's first sip from a cup. In a lifetime Mary could never express all the ways she experienced God.

Luke 2:19 records a mother's practice, "Mary treasured up all these things and pondered them in her heart." She held on to each moment for dear life. The word *pondered* is *sumballo* which describes taking many things, casting them together and considering them as one.[13] Mary held the Christ child close to her breast and allowed her mind to drift over the events of the past year: her humble home, the sudden appearance and divine proclamation of the angel, her departure to Elizabeth's, her parents' faces when she told them the news, the rumors, Joseph's reaction, the way she felt when he believed the angel and came for her. The miserable journey to Bethlehem. The first pains of labor. The fear of having no place to give birth. The pain. The joy.

Each experience making up the whole. What held them together as one? The faithfulness of God. He was intimately involved in every piece of the puzzle.

What brings you to this place today? Like Mary, God brought you to this point through a blend of pleasure and pain, faith and sight, questions and certainties. For a few moments reflect on the major events God pieced together to bring you to this point in your spiritual journey. Meditate on the last 10 years of your life. Identify five major puzzle pieces God has joined together to make you who and what you are today.

To appreciate God's work in our lives through pleasure and pain, we must understand that He thinks in terms of the whole. Of completeness. Of pieces that finally fit together as one. Life's a little easier when we adopt His perspective. *Sumballo.*

Look at each piece of your life as part of a whole. Has God been faithful? Then treasure these things. And ponder them in your heart.

Praise

....

....

....

....

....

....

Repentance

....

....

....

....

....

Acknowledgment

....

....

....

....

....

Intercession

....

....

....

....

....

Supplication for Self

....

....

....

....

....

Equipping

....

....

....

....

....

NICHOLAS PAVLOFF

Day Sixty-One

*"As they were walking along and talking together, suddenly a chariot of fire
and horses of fire appeared and separated the two of them,
and Elijah went up to heaven in a whirlwind" (2 Kings 2:11).*

Scripture Reading: 2 Kings 2:1-18

If you've been a serving believer long, you've probably enjoyed the tutelage of an
"Elijah." I certainly have. "Elijahs" are precious gifts from God to nurture us in our
spiritual lives. We see them as God's favored ones. Those we believe have a special
"in" with God. They are our heroes. The ones we look up to and call in times of crisis. Their most important role, however, is discipleship—not dependency, and that's
why our "Elijahs" are usually only temporary.

Some of us feel hurt or bitter because we're not as close to this person as we used
to be. We don't understand what changed. We don't want to let go of what we had.

Elisha struggled terribly with the changing nature of his relationship with Elijah.
His tutor was his strength. He could not imagine serving without Elijah by his side.
Elisha was so frightened he was going to lose Elijah that he followed him everywhere.
Over and over the young servant echoed, "I will not leave you" (2 Kings 2:2,4,6).

I wonder if Elisha really meant, "Promise you won't leave me!" Sometimes we
lack the power to make those promises. Many tried to warn Elisha to prepare for the
separation, but he refused to listen. Finally, when forced to hear the truth, Elisha had
only one request: "Let me inherit a double portion of your spirit" (2 Kings 2:9). He
asked the blessing of a firstborn son, and God tenderly granted his request.

No matter how badly Elisha wanted to hang on to Elijah, separation was
inevitable. The results reveal why God usually retains our Elijahs only temporarily.
Look at Elisha's response in verse 14: "Where now is the Lord, the God of Elijah?"

You see, Elisha had attached the presence of the Lord in his life to the presence of
Elijah. Without his mentor, how would he ever find God? He even called God the
"God of Elijah." How would Elisha ever discover that God was his own if Elijah
retained his powerfully influential role in the young man's life?

God isn't likely to sweep your Elijah up in a whirlwind, but a change in the relationship is virtually inevitable. We don't give babies crutches. We teach them to walk.
When God sees we are ready to walk, often He places some distance between us and
the person we're dependent on. He wants to show us He is our God, too.

Sometimes we must give up our Elijahs, but like Elisha, we get to keep one treasure
forever: the cloak they left behind. Everything we learned from them. Each memory.
The heritage of their faithfulness. That's our cloak.

Don't despise the cloak because it's all you have left. The cloak was God's intention
all along.

Praise

....

....

....

....

....

....

Repentance

....

....

....

....

....

Acknowledgment

....

....

....

....

....

Intercession

Supplication for Self

Equipping

Day Sixty-Two

"But we have the mind of Christ" (1 Cor. 2:16).

Scripture Reading: 1 Corinthians 2:11-16; 3:1

Paul made a revolutionary—almost inconceivable—statement in his first letter to the Corinthians. He told them, "we have the mind of Christ."

Interestingly, Paul was addressing worldly believers who refused to grow up. You see, the gift of the mind of Christ is given to every believer, regardless of whether or not we ever acknowledge or use it. When we received Christ, the Holy Spirit took up residence in our lives. He left no part of Himself behind. Remember, the Holy Spirit is a person. He moved in with invisible "feet" so He could direct us in our walk with God; with "hands" so He could slip them through ours and empower us to serve; with His heart so He could stir passion within us and equip us with supernatural love.

Contrary to some popular thinking, however, the Holy Spirit is not just a doing and feeling presence within us. He also provides the brains behind the operation. He moves in with the mind of Christ.

Those who have received Christ have the capacity to comprehend God's truths. We have the ability to process information too complicated for the brightest intellectual. We possess an innate creativity beyond the most gifted artist. We have a potential for understanding beyond the wisest counselor. We have the mind of Christ.

We also continue to possess the mind of the flesh just as we still possess natural bodies though we've become spiritual creatures. We still possess our old ways of thinking. We are double-minded persons, challenged daily to choose which realm will prevail. One day we may think like Christ and the next like the old man of sin.

What are we to do? Verse 14 holds the key. The things of the Spirit provoke the thoughts of the Spirit. When we "accept the things that come from the Spirit of God," we begin to discern truths beyond the natural mind. God's Word, prayer, and godly people are things of the Spirit. They provoke thinking with the mind of Christ.

The more we partake of the things of the Spirit, the more we begin to think like the Spirit: loving what He loves, hating what He hates, grieving over what hurts Him, rejoicing over what thrills Him. Understanding will sometimes come to us without adequate words to express it—spiritual truths with no physical words. We feel differently because we think differently. These are evidences of the mind of Christ within us.

Beloved, fathom the miracle of it. We are finite beings of frail human flesh occupied by the Spirit of the supernatural, all-powerful, all-present, all-knowing Godhead. Inconceivable—unless you're thinking with the mind of Christ.

Let's begin asking God daily to quicken the mind of Christ in us so that, like the great apostle Paul, we can supernaturally understand "what God has freely given us." Oh, how life will change.

Praise

....

....

....

....

....

....

Repentance

....

....

....

....

....

Acknowledgment

....

....

....

....

....

Intercession

....

....

....

....

....

....

Supplication for Self

....

....

....

....

....

....

Equipping

....

....

....

....

....

J.D. MARSTON

Day Sixty-Three

"Peacemakers who sow in peace raise a harvest of righteousness" (Jas. 3:18).

Scripture Reading: James 3:13–4:1

Biblical peacemakers are not those who live in denial or with ulcerated stomachs from trying to keep everyone happy. Biblical peacemakers are people personally at peace with God's authority and willing to bring a presence of peace to their surroundings. This world could use a few more healthy peacemakers.

James 4:1 asks a compelling question: "What causes fights and quarrels among you?" Conflict is an undeniable part of the human condition. To some degree it exists in every church, home, and workplace. It does not always have to result in fights and quarrels, but it often does because people are resistant to assuming responsibility for their personal contributions to the conflict.

I fear that a tendency prevalent today is crippling our ability to take responsibility for our own actions. The trend is to blame somebody else for our behavior. We seem to believe that "everything wrong with me is someone else's fault."

Recently I was frustrated with someone who repeatedly forgot to submit some information I needed for a Bible study. I genuinely like this person so I tried and tried to be patient while the deadline rushed toward me. Finally, I was irritated because he placed me in the position to have to confront him.

When I finally mustered the courage, the man's response totally disarmed me. He looked me straight in the face and said, "I'm sorry, Beth. I blew it." I was so shocked at his no-excuses apology, every bit of the anger drained from me. I grinned and said, "That's okay. I bet we can fix it."

For days I thought about his response and decided I want to be the kind of person who can immediately say "I'm sorry." No excuses.

One crucial way for us to become agents of peace is to assume responsibility for our own mistakes—for our contributions to conflict. Reread James 3:13. The writer reminds us that the one "who is wise and understanding" will show it "by deeds done in the humility that comes from wisdom." Saying we're sorry requires humility. By human nature, we don't want others to know we're ever wrong. We want to look good. Wisdom finally teaches us that those who take responsibility for their mistakes and can say the words "I'm sorry" without choking are the ones who don't just look good—they are good. James 3:18 says they "raise a harvest of righteousness."

I've found that those two troublesome words "I'm sorry" are not nearly so hard to say if I spit them out quickly. The longer I wait, the worse they taste. Start practicing this week. Say it to your children if you're grouchy. Say it to a coworker if you didn't follow through. Say it to your friend if you've left them waiting.

Say it. Say it. Say it. And sow a little peace.

Praise

....

....

....

....

....

....

Repentance

....

....

....

....

....

....

Acknowledgment

....

....

....

....

....

Intercession

....

....

....

....

....

Supplication for Self

....

....

....

....

....

Equipping

....

....

....

....

....

Day Sixty-Four

"Join with others in following my example, brothers and take note of those who live according to the pattern we gave you" (Phil. 3:17).

Scripture Reading: Philippians 3:17-21

In July 1969 we observed an incredible event. We sat in stunned silence as man set foot on the moon. Neil Armstrong wore the first boots to ever disturb lunar dust.

Armstrong was an unlikely candidate for the honor; he was the first civilian to enter the astronaut training program. After his history-making trip, he never returned to the moon. But it didn't really matter. Today his footprints remain. The moon has no wind nor rain to displace them. Until God, Himself, blows them away, Armstrong's steps are safely established on that distant surface.

On the planet Earth, we have no such conditions. Here footprints don't last long. The apostle Paul left footprints bronzed in the Word of God, but through the Spirit's inspiration, he calls on others to leave marks for future sojourners to follow.

Over and over in Scripture God calls His people to be faithful to teach all generations His principles. He doesn't just call on parents to teach their children. He entrusts the entire present generation of His people with the calling to teach those who follow.

None of us will argue that the next generation is at great risk. Our youth are unlikely to open the pages of Scripture and follow the apostle's example unless they've been personally challenged by a living, breathing example of one "walking the walk."

Many past men and women left "marks" for others to follow. For some of us, Tozer, Corrie Ten Boom, and Spurgeon are familiar names, but few young people know these authors. The winds of time are blowing. Their faithful footprints are fading—just as God planned. He has not given us the luxury of depending on giants of the past. God wants fresh prints left by every generation for the next to follow. Now it's our turn. Our youth are desperate for examples of passionate, authentic believers.

Can you think of a few good candidates to leave fresh prints? Forget them. I'm asking you. Will you step out in faith, become more visible and deliberate, and allow your feet to leave footsteps others can follow to Christ?

I don't suppose Neil Armstrong felt especially adequate to leave the first prints on the moon. When Billy Graham met with his first president, he probably felt inadequate to advise the most powerful man in the world. While Mother Theresa gazed at India's endless sea of poverty, I can't imagine she felt very adequate to help. But each of these individuals left prints that continue to deeply affect their generations.

We don't have to begin by doing something outstanding. Just start by being more deliberate about setting godly examples. It is not our responsibility to look behind and see who's following. It is our responsibility to leave prints worth following.

Go ahead! Stir up a little dust. Those boots are made for walkin'.

Praise

....
....
....
....
....
....

Repentance

....
....
....
....
....

Acknowledgment

....
....
....
....
....

Intercession

....

....

....

....

....

Supplication for Self

....

....

....

....

....

Equipping

....

....

....

....

NICHOLAS PAVLOFF

Day Sixty-Five

"Like a madman shooting firebrands or deadly arrows is a man who deceives his neighbor and says, 'I was only joking!'" (Prov. 26:18-19).

Scripture Reading: Proverbs 26:18-19; James 3:2-6

Sticks and stones may break my bones, but words will never hurt me." Whoever first said that—lied. Most people are able to forget broken bones sooner than scalding words.

We can each remember being hurt by a careless or hurtful word. Worse yet, we can remember hurting someone else by something we said. We may have been instantly sorry. We may not have even meant what we said. Or perhaps we did, but we certainly didn't mean for the person we spoke about to hear it.

Our mouths get away from us like runaway trains—with similar results. One minute we're the center of attention; we're blowing and going. The next thing you know, the targeted person learns what we said. Like the writer of Proverbs 26, we sometimes claim, "I was only joking!" Maybe. But the person hurt never forgets he or she was the punch line.

God's Word says that the one who can tame her tongue is the one able to bridle the whole body. In fact, if we read the James passage carefully, we can safely deduce that a tamed tongue is one of the chief characteristics of a mature Christian. Why is it that this oral cavern of ours is one of the last frontiers we allow Christ to conquer?

Left outside the Spirit's control, the tongue is dangerous. Words rub together like sticks. A spark bursts into flame and, as others catch on, the flame quickly escalates to forest fire status. A destructive game of one-upmanship commences as we fan one another's flames. Someone will surely get burned. Wounds don't heal easily—or quickly—and often scars result.

In the last several days, I've noted that three different people in unrelated conversations repeated words someone said to them years ago. In each case the words still sting. That's the problem with fires. New growth is a long time coming.

Sadly, Christians don't differ much from the rest of the world in matters of the tongue. James 3:9 says, "With the tongue we praise our Lord and Father, and with it we curse men, who have been made in God's likeness." Many times we criticize the preacher before we even get to our cars on Sunday after the worship service.

The Word of God says the tongue is a tattletale. "For out of the overflow of his heart his mouth speaks" (Luke 6:45). In other words, our speech reveals our heart.

Let's allow God to get to the heart of the matter and to heal us of our verbal pyromania. These are hard words, but a fiery tongue is not easily quenched.

Today, allow God to use His Word like a bucket of water.

Praise

....

....

....

....

....

....

Repentance

....

....

....

....

....

Acknowledgment

....

....

....

....

Intercession

....

....

....

....

....

....

Supplication for Self

....

....

....

....

....

....

Equipping

....

....

....

....

....

Day Sixty-Six

"If one part suffers, every part suffers with it; if one part is honored, every part rejoices with it" (1 Cor. 12:26).

Scripture Reading: 1 Corinthians 12:21-27

Part of our "body" is suffering—I mean really suffering. Many knowledgeable observers are convinced we are presently living in the greatest era of Christian persecution in all history. Shocking, isn't it? Never before have so many Christians been persecuted for their beliefs. An estimated 200 million to 250 million Christians are at risk. Because they are so far removed from our day-to-day experience, we often don't acknowledge these Christians' place in the body.[14]

Several alarming new books contain eyewitness testimonies of terrible suffering by Christians at the hands of persecutors. While we sometimes experience mild forms of persecution like being overlooked for promotions at work, in other countries believers in horrifying numbers are being imprisoned, tortured, and executed. Children are sometimes taken from believing parents as punishment for their faith. These children are forced to be slaves—or worse. In our present generation, people whose names we'll never know have endured broken limbs and scalded skin for refusing to renounce the name of Christ.

The Lamb's book of life records hundreds of thousands of faithful followers who have given their lives for the cause of Christ. My heart broke with conviction as I read the words of an American Jewish lawyer who is doing everything he can to alert influential people about this persecution. His memory of the Nazi crimes against the Jews fuels his concern for persecuted Christians. He cannot comprehend why American Christians seem out of touch and uninvolved with their fellow disciples. We can offer one reason, but we can't excuse our lack of concern; we are uninformed.

These suffering believers are our brothers and sisters in Christ. Colossians 2:19 tells us Christ is "the Head, from whom the whole body, supported and held together by its ligaments and sinews, grows as God causes it to grow." Praise God, the "body" is growing, but it is suffering from torn ligaments. Our "connectors" are weak. How can the ligaments be strengthened? The key is PRAYER!

Oh, that God would increase our sense of connection to believers around the world! They are part of us. Many are suffering terribly. Will we allow them to permeate our thoughts and cost us a tear or two? We can take our concern to the floor of intercession and stand in the gap for them. Christ will act as a direct result of intercessory prayer. We will spend eternity with these people. One day they will know we cared. We will hear their testimonies and surely think, "The world was not worthy of them" (Heb. 11:38).

Beloved, make it a priority to be informed. Care. Pray. Strengthen the ligaments.

Praise

....

....

....

....

....

....

Repentance

....

....

....

....

....

Acknowledgment

....

....

....

....

....

Intercession

....

....

....

....

....

....

Supplication for Self

....

....

....

....

....

Equipping

....

....

....

....

....

J.D. MARSTON

Day Sixty-Seven

"Then, because so many people were coming and going that they did not even have a chance to eat, he said to them,'Come with me by yourselves to a quiet place and get some rest'" (Mark 6:31).

Scripture Reading: Mark 6:7-13,30-32

We discover great wisdom in knowing when to retreat with God. I'm not talking about a prayer retreat dedicated to intense intercession or a believer's conference dedicated to deepening spiritual growth. Although both examples enhance our spiritual maturity, I'm speaking of a different kind of retreat—the "original" retreat.

The disciples had been on the road preaching, driving out demons, anointing the sick with oil, and healing people in Jesus' name. Although their ventures were successful, Christ looked past their adrenaline and into their exhaustion. He spoke some of my favorite words in the Gospel of Mark: "Come with me by yourselves to a quiet place and get some rest."

Jesus wasn't just talking about a nap. The original Greek word for *rest* is *anapauo* which means "to give rest, quiet, recreate, refresh."[15] He was talking about a nap plus a game of volleyball in the sand, or a barefooted walk through a creek, or a glass of lemonade accompanied by fun stories and a few laughs, or a walk by themselves, or a simple talk not meant to change the world. RECREATION. Servant of God, occasionally you've just got to have it—in Jesus' name.

I don't think our text is necessarily talking about a ski trip with the relatives—although God certainly honors a good family vacation. Our Scriptures today relate times when Christ calls hard-working servants aside to recreate with Him and in Him. This kind of recreation differs from a vacation. The distinction may be hard to define, but it is pretty easy to discern. Mark 6:30-32 describes refreshment with spiritual results—a deeper appreciation for God, an acute awareness of His presence, a sense of His approval, a bask in His love.

Would you like to hear some really good news? Christ's call to recreation doesn't come just once in a lifetime. Look back at the original Greek word for *rest*. Those first three letters, *ana*, mean "again." In other words, Christ called His disciples to rest, recreate, and find refreshment in Him again!

As we serve Him with all of our hearts, Christ will intermittently woo us to a place of rest and refreshment. We don't have to preach from village to village, cast out demons, and heal the sick to qualify for a little refreshment. God honors our whole-hearted willingness to serve Him in whatever capacity He has appointed.

When we're exhausted, God calls us to rest. We need only to grant ourselves a little permission. God doesn't work us into the ground. He desires us well-grounded in our work. Knowing when to retreat helps define the difference.

Praise

....
....
....
....
....
....

Repentance

....
....
....
....
....
....

Acknowledgment

....
....
....
....
....

Intercession

....

....

....

....

....

....

Supplication for Self

....

....

....

....

....

....

Equipping

....

....

....

....

....

....

Day Sixty-Eight

"You have made my days a mere handbreadth; the span of my years is as nothing before you. Each man's life is but a breath" (Ps. 39:5).

Scripture Reading: Psalm 39

David practiced what he preached. In Psalm 62:8, he exhorted the children of God to "pour out your hearts to him, for God is our refuge." David wasn't one to keep his feelings to himself. He was a marvelous blend of passion and expression; therefore, what he felt—he usually said. Psalm 39 is a perfect example. He even begins the psalm by vocalizing the miseries of remaining mute. Questions and frustrations concerning God had overwhelmed him until "the fire burned" in his heart and "[he] spoke with [his] tongue" (v. 3). The remainder of the psalm records David's troubled thoughts. He loved and trusted his God so thoroughly, he knew he would not be cast away for spilling the painful overflow of his heart.

The theme of his passion in this particular text was the fragility of life. When was the last time you were reminded how fragile life is? Chances are, the circumstances were upsetting and likely involved the loss of someone's life. We have no way of knowing what sparked David's sudden and strong emotions about life's frailties, but when the spark turned into a roaring fire, he knew God could take the heat. His burning heart boiled forth with the words: "You have made my days a mere handbreadth; the span of my years is as nothing before you. Each man's life is but a breath."

David was right about the brevity of life, but he was wrong if he believed each millisecond of his life did not tick like a metronome in God's heart. Indeed, our lives are a handbreadth—but not a mere handbreadth. More importantly perhaps, our lives are not man's handbreadth, but God's. In every sense of the word, our lives are in God's hands.

- Psalm 37:24 says, "though he stumble, he will not fall, for the Lord upholds him with his hand."
- Psalm 139:9-10 says, "If I rise on the wings of the dawn, if I settle on the far side of the sea, even there your hand will guide me, your right hand will hold me fast."
- Isaiah 49:16 says, "See, I have engraved you on the palms of my hands."
- Exodus 33:22 says, "When my glory passes by, I will put you in a cleft in the rock and cover you with my hand."

Yes, our lives are a handbreadth—God's handbreadth. We have His thumbprint on us the moment we're conceived and the imprint of His little finger the moment we leave. Every moment in between, we're covered by His love. Every moment of our belief, we're covered by His blood. And when the last breath is drawn, if we are His own, He wraps His arms around our lives and takes us safely home.

Praise

....

....

....

....

....

....

Repentance

....

....

....

....

....

Acknowledgment

....

....

....

....

....

Intercession

....

....

....

....

....

Supplication for Self

....

....

....

....

....

Equipping

....

....

....

....

....

NICHOLAS PAVLOFF

Day Sixty-Nine

"Who am I, O Sovereign Lord...that you have brought me this far?" (2 Sam. 7:18).

Scripture Reading: 2 Samuel 7:1-22

In our Christian quest to go farther, we tend to overlook how far we've come. Few things de-motivate like trying to move forward when you feel as if you've never budged. When was the last time your eyes were suddenly opened to a glimpse of growth? Savoring a sudden realization of progress with the One who gave it is gloriously appropriate! God wants you to celebrate progress with Him just as David did.

David's response to God's goodness reveals obvious reasons why he was a man after God's own heart (see 1 Sam. 13:14). No wonder David was the apple of God's eye! (see Ps. 17:8.) When we passionately surrender our hearts to God, the realization of how far we've come should spark similar responses in us. Let's highlight a few:

Intimacy: Notice David sought no other audience. He left Nathan's presence and "went in and sat before the Lord" (v. 18). Before we celebrate God's unexpected blessings with others—those with hearts "after His own"—seek Him first.

Humility: Should the thought of celebrating progress with God seem arrogant? Only if we're taking the credit! David was completely humbled by God's goodness. He didn't even stand in God's presence as he celebrated. We show pride when we flaunt our gains like multicolored coats before those who don't yet have them.

Regard for God's Sovereignty: Notice the fitting title David attributed to God: "O Sovereign Lord!" Psalm 115:3 appropriately describes God's sovereignty: "Our God is in heaven; he does whatever pleases him." David's approach to God revealed the attitude of his heart: "By Your sovereignty, I'm where I am today. I will take no credit."

Delight: All of us enjoy doing something special for someone who responds not only with gratitude, but also with excitement! Can you imagine how blessed God's heart is when we are stunned and thrilled over His goodness? Our delight in His awesome work tenders His heart and makes us a joy to bless.

Acknowledgment: Perhaps one of God's chief goals is to bring us to a place where we joyfully exclaim: "How great you are, O Sovereign Lord! There is no one like you!"

Have you reached the place where you can sincerely and personally make the declaration, "God, there is none like You!"? Then, Beloved, no matter where you've been, you've come "so far." Spend some time with your blessed Sovereign Lord today. Sit before Him and celebrate "that He has brought you this far." Reflect on His goodness—His countless rescues—His tender mercies. Let Him show you a few signs of your own progress. Can you remember not so long ago when worship and His Word were not priorities? Revel in a little freedom from self absorption.

You've come so far.

Celebrate. You are the apple of His eye.

Praise

....

....

....

....

....

....

Repentance

....

....

....

....

....

....

Acknowledgment

....

....

....

....

....

....

Intercession

....

....

....

....

....

Supplication for Self

....

....

....

....

....

Equipping

....

....

....

....

....

Day Seventy

"When they had all had enough to eat, he said to his disciples, 'Gather the pieces that are left over. Let nothing be wasted'" (John 6:12).

Scripture reading: John 6:1-15

Millions of people on this planet are starving to death—literally and spiritually. We can and should give to relief efforts that feed the poor, but something even greater is at stake: souls hungry for the Bread of life. Because God never wills anyone to perish, He placed within each person an inner man, a spirit hungry for God.

The hungry and hurting multitudes may not be able to voice what they need, but we can. We must spread the message of salvation. We must teach the Word of God. Our generation has been entrusted to us.

Today approximately six billion people walk, toddle, or crawl on this earth. Although one billion of those call themselves Christians, a far lesser number are born-again, Bible-believing Christians. God knows the exact number of those who call Jesus Lord. He has made them ambassadors of Christ, charging them with offering the Bread of life to all people in all nations. But how can a few reach out to so many?

In effect, Christ asked the same question of Philip in John 6:5 when the few were faced with feeding many. "Where shall we buy bread for these people to eat?" The next verse is crucial: "He asked this only to test him, for he already had in mind what he was going to do." Sometimes Christ places a question in our minds to make us seek Him for the answer.

Our question today is: "How will you obey Me and reach out to the multitudes?"

Like Philip, we feel ill-equipped, outnumbered, and intimidated. Often we feel so overwhelmed by such a worldwide task that we don't even try. Yet Christ already has in mind how He wants to feed the multitudes—the same way He fed them in John 6.

A miracle occurs every single time one solitary person offers everything he or she has to Christ. You may think you have so little to give, but if you surrender your all to Him, ultimately He will touch multitudes in ways you may never know.

In Acts 5, Ananias and Sapphira stood (or shall I say "dropped"?) in such stark contrast to the boy with the five small barley loaves and two small fish. They had so much yet offered so little. He had so little yet offered all he had. And Christ blessed it and multiplied it many times over. He'll do it every time.

The feeding of the five thousand account concludes with Christ's words, "Let nothing be wasted" (v. 12). Beloved, when you surrender yourself entirely to Christ, nothing will be wasted. Not one aggravation. Not one tribulation. Not one celebration. Not one single breath of your life.

One day, when God gathers each of us in His arms, may He be able to say, "This child withheld nothing from me." A life without waste. Make haste.

Praise

....

....

....

....

....

Repentance

....

....

....

....

....

Acknowledgment

....

....

....

....

Intercession

....

....

....

....

....

Supplication for Self

....

....

....

....

....

Equipping

....

....

....

....

....

Answered Prayers

Answered Prayers

Answered Prayers

Answered Prayers

Answered Prayers

Endnotes

1. *The Complete Word Study Old Testament* (Chattanooga, TN: AMG Publishers, 1994), 2341.
2. Spiros Zodhiates et al., eds., *The Complete Word Study Dictionary: New Testament* (Chattanooga, TN: AMG Publishers, 1992), 921, 1154.
3. Ibid., 920.
4. Ibid., 299.
5. Ibid., 457.
6. Ibid.
7. James Strong, *The Exhaustive Concordance of the Bible* (Nashville: Holman Bible Publishers, n.d.), 100.
8. Oswald Chambers, *He Shall Glorify Me* (London: Oswald Chambers Publications Association, 1946), 134.
9. Spiros Zodhiates, *The Complete Word Study Dictionary: New Testament*, 864.
10. Ibid., 593-594.
11. Ibid., 62.
12. Ibid., 551.
13. Ibid., 1326.
14. Paul Marshall, *Their Blood Cries Out* (Dallas: Word Publishing, 1997), 4.
15. Spiros Zodhiates, *The Complete Word Study Dictionary: New Testament*, 156.

Group Study Plan

Prayer and journaling are daily and personal activities, but you can greatly enhance your experience by meeting weekly with a group of prayer partners. Making this prayer journey together produces extra benefits of greater spiritual growth, understanding, accountability, and encouragement.

Because no one best way exists to conduct a *Whispers of Hope* group, I am suggesting some principles and options for a group study plan. Choose the approach and type of structure that will help you and your group members build a faithful prayer life. You will need to clarify two basic issues. First, what level of accountability will the group practice? Second, will the group's focus be on prayer, or will you combine prayer with review of the material for the week?

The Issue of Accountability

The accountability of a group helps members maintain their commitment to a growing devotional life. The very fact that the group meets can help many of us develop faithfulness and spend time with Christ. I strongly believe in a system of accountability. I need sisters who will pointedly ask me about my commitments and my devotional life.

You will have people who struggle with consistency in their prayer lives. We have a much easier time getting out of bed and bending the knee if we know we will be asked to give an account of our faithfulness. I encourage your group to talk frankly at the first meeting and settle on the degree of accountability members will expect from one another. The group can encourage each member to develop the discipline of daily prayer by practicing one of the levels of accountability described below.

Group Accountability: Accountability can be a regular function of the group meeting. Every member knows that as a regular part of the meeting she will briefly report her successes and struggles with having a quiet time, prayer, and journal experience daily.

Accountability Partners: To increase the level of accountability, divide the group into pairs. Each person will have an accountability partner. As a regular part of each weekly meeting, plan a time for accountability partners to report to each other their faithfulness and struggles with a regular prayer time.

Accountability partners plus a daily phone call: For the most powerful level of accountability, divide into pairs with the understanding that partners will call each other daily. In addition to confirming their quiet times, partners can pray together over the phone. In group sessions partners can pray together, or you may have a group accountability report as in the first suggestion above.

Leading a *Whispers of Hope* Group

First, last, and always—pray for your group and your leadership. God may guide you to lead the group in some way totally different from my recommendations. You can use some or all of these recommendations in your group. Concentrate on two areas: be sensitive to the Holy Spirit and what He is leading the group to do, and be sensitive to the needs of your group. What would help group members develop a strong relationship with Christ?

Whispers of Hope is a daily prayer journal. My purpose in writing has been to help women develop more effective prayer lives. Decide if your group will emphasize prayer or prayer and study. Simply getting together without a clearly-determined group purpose invites trouble. My experience with groups suggests that you need to determine the focus of the group.

If you have a group of disciplined prayer warriors, consider prayer as the single purpose of your group. Such a group will get together to spend the time praying. The focus will not be on study or review. In fact, you will want to avoid taking away from time spent in prayer. Your group will simply meet and pray. Beware of distractions that draw you away from prayer. Don't spend the time talking about prayer...PRAY!

If you want more suggestions for a group with the primary purpose of prayer, read *In God's Presence,* by T.W. Hunt and Claude King (ISBN 0-7673-0001-7). If you opt for a pure prayer group, you can largely disregard my suggestions for a study format. If you will combine prayer and study, choose from among the following approaches:

A Content-Centered Group: Lead the group to discuss some of the ways God has spoken to members this week through the meditations and journaling. Each day's meditation deals with a different theme. Without re-reading the meditations in the group, review the theme of each day. You can quickly remind yourself of the theme by reading the first and last few lines of most lessons. Spend a few minutes discussing each meditation. Ask questions such as:

- "In what way does this message challenge your thinking or behavior?"
- "How does this issue impact your relationship with Christ?"
- "What do you need to do in response to this message?"

You may find that your group will automatically have plenty to talk about for the meeting time. Seek to keep the focus on what they are learning and on what God is doing in their lives.

A Format-Centered Group: Focus each week on a different aspect of the P.R.A.I.S.E. format: P(raise), R(epent), A(cknowledging His authority), I(ntercession), S(upplication), and E(quipping).

You can formulate group discussion questions for each area or use standard questions like the following. In subsequent weeks, substitute repenting of sin, acknowledging His authority, etc. for praise:

1. What impact has praise had on your relationship to God this week?
2. When did praise first become a regular part of your relationship to God?
3. Describe your most significant experience with praise.
4. In what ways do you need to grow in praising God?
5. What benefits do you experience from regularly praising God?

An Application-Centered Group: This approach focuses on applying to life the week's study and prayer with special emphasis on becoming equipped for ministry and service. Explain to members that during group sessions each of you will share how God has been equipping you during the week. As in the content-centered group, briefly review the theme for each day, but review them with an emphasis on the last of the journal sections. Ask:

1. How is God using this concept, principle, or truth to equip you to live a more Christ-honoring life?
2. How is He using this idea to equip you for more effective service?
3. In this area of life, what do you need to be what Christ intends?

As you participate in a group, I pray that you will develop a deeper love, trust, and obedience relationship with Christ. May you grow in understanding, but, more importantly, may you fall more and more deeply in love with our Savior. One day may we each reach the place where we would sacrifice anything rather than miss our time with Him.

About the Author

Beth Moore realized at the age of 18 that God was claiming her future for Christian ministry. While she was sponsoring a cabin of sixth graders at a missions camp, God unmistakably acknowledged that she would work for Him. There Beth conceded all rights to the Lord she had loved since childhood. However, she encountered a problem: although she knew she was "wonderfully made," she was "fearfully" without talent. She hid behind closed doors to discover whether a beautiful singing voice had miraculously developed, but the results were tragic. She returned to the piano from which years of fruitless practice had streamed but found the noise to be joyless. Finally accepting that the only remaining alternative was missions work in a foreign country, she struck a martyr's pose and waited. Yet nothing happened.

Still confident of God's calling, Beth finished her degree at Southwest Texas State University, where she fell in love with Keith. After they married in December 1978, God added to their household three priority blessings: Amanda, Melissa, and Michael.

As if putting together puzzle pieces one at a time, God filled Beth's path with supportive persons who saw something in her she could not. God used individuals like Marge Caldwell, John Bisagno, and Jeannette Cliff George to help Beth discover gifts of speaking, teaching, and writing. Twelve years after her first speaking engagement, those gifts have spread all over the nation. Her joy and excitement in Christ are contagious; her deep love for the Savior, obvious; her style of speaking, electric.

Beth's ministry is grounded in and fueled by her service at her home fellowship, First Baptist Church, Houston, Texas, where she serves on the pastor's council and teaches a Sunday School class attended by more than two hundred women. Beth believes that her calling is Bible literacy: guiding believers to love and live God's Word. She loves the Lord, loves to laugh, and loves to be with His people. Her life is full of activity, but one commitment remains constant: counting all things but loss for the excellence of knowing Christ Jesus, the Lord (see Phil. 3:8).

In-depth Bible studies
from Beth Moore

❧ To Live Is Christ: The Life and Ministry of Paul

Join Beth Moore on an expedition through Scripture to learn more about the amazing life and ministry of the Apostle Paul. Discover why Paul said, "To live is Christ, and to die is gain." As you study these passages you will come to know the characters personally. Most of all you will feel the challenge to follow Paul's example just as he followed the example of Christ.

❧ A Heart Like His: Seeking the Heart of God Through A Study of David

Discover how you can be a woman after God's own heart as you learn more about King David, the man after God's own heart. You'll experience the ups and downs of the shepherd king, and you'll come to love his God in a new way. Although David lived thousands of years ago, he dealt with many of the same issues which trouble God's people today. If you've ever had doubts, fought temptations, fallen into sin, suffered losses, or anguished over family problems, then this Bible study is for you!

❧ A Woman's Heart: God's Dwelling Place

Why would a holy God want to dwell among His people? Explore the fascinating account of the building of the Old Testament tabernacle in *A Woman's Heart: God's Dwelling Place*. Discover the significance of the tabernacle's intricate design, its pivotal role in God's plan, the grand fulfillment of its purpose by Jesus Christ, and its variety of meanings for your walk with God.

❧ Resources for each 11-week study include a member book, leader guide,* audiocassette tapes, and a video-driven leader kit.

The leader kit contains five videotapes featuring author and speaker Beth Moore as she presents lessons from the Scriptures, and a sixth videotape with a leadership, administrative, and promotional segment. In addition the kit contains one member book and leader guide.*included in *A Heart Like His* member book

Order by calling 1-800-458-2772 or visit your Baptist Book Store or Lifeway Christian store.